THE QUICK AND EASY WICKED GOOD MUFFINS COOKBOOK

TULLUAR BERTLATY

INTRODUCTION

Welcome to "The Quick and Easy Wicked Good Muffins Cookbook"! The very title of this book may evoke a sense of curiosity, tinged with a hint of excitement. Indeed, the aroma of freshly baked muffins wafting through your home is a universally cherished scent, capable of conjuring memories of simple joys and shared moments. This cookbook is here to take you on a unique gastronomical journey, a rollercoaster ride packed with a kaleidoscope of flavors, textures, and aromas. From classic and fruit-based muffins to the fun and innovative varieties, the muffin empire is rich, diverse, and waiting to be explored.

In this book, we present a comprehensive array of recipes, each meticulously curated, experimented, and tested to perfection, for every occasion, taste, and dietary preference. We begin our adventure with the 'Classic Flavors', chapter one, an homage to the timeless and universally loved tastes like vanilla, chocolate, and caramel. These recipes cater to the muffin traditionalists among us, as well as those starting their baking journey. These muffins have withstood the test of time and emerged as favorites across generations, regions, and cultures.

We progress to 'Fruit-Based Muffins' in the second

chapter, where we infuse these delectable treats with a fruity freshness that livens up our palates. This section is brimming with the vibrant tastes of lemon, blueberry, cherry, pear, and many more. Each muffin promises to burst with natural sweetness and unique flavors that will delight your senses and take you on a trip to the fruit orchard.

Next up, 'Fun Flavors'. This chapter aims to push boundaries and broaden your culinary horizons. From Nutella™ and Funfetti to Mocha and Maple Bacon, these muffins showcase a fusion of flavors that will surely dazzle your taste buds. These recipes embody the spirit of creativity and experimentation, making them perfect for those adventurous bakers ready to discover a new dimension of muffin-making.

Chapter four brings us to 'Veggie-Based Muffins'. These recipes offer a clever way of sneaking some nutritious greens into your meals. Carrot, zucchini, and pumpkin have been disguised as mouth-watering muffins, retaining their nutrients but adding a dash of indulgence. It's time to let your garden join in on your baking escapades!

We are mindful of those with dietary restrictions, and we have dedicated an entire chapter to 'Gluten-Free Muffins'. This section ensures that everyone can join the muffin party, regardless of their dietary needs. From blueberry to banana walnut, and vanilla to creamy chocolate, these gluten-free versions are no less delicious than their classic counterparts.

Finally, we conclude with 'Savory Muffins' in the sixth chapter. These savory treats offer a delightful break from the sugary sweetness, injecting a wave of rich, satisfying flavors. Imagine sinking your teeth into a fluffy muffin loaded with zucchini and bacon, broccoli and cheese, or spinach and egg. These muffins make a perfect breakfast or brunch treat, adding a fun twist to your usual savory meals.

The variety of recipes in this book ensures that every reader, regardless of their skill level or preference, will find a muffin that speaks to their heart. The goal of this book is not just to provide you with a list of recipes; it's an invitation to the world of muffins, to embrace the joy of baking, and to find pleasure in the simplest things. Whether you are an amateur baker who is taking their first steps into the world of pastries or a professional who knows their way around the kitchen, this book promises to be a trusty companion on your baking journey.

In the pages that follow, we've meticulously provided instructions to ensure every muffin-making experience becomes a delightful adventure. Each recipe is adorned with hints and tips to navigate potential pitfalls and troubleshoot any issues that may arise during your baking experience. We also detail the exact measurements, oven temperatures, and baking times to guarantee your muffins come out perfectly every time.

More than just a cookbook, "The Quick and Easy Wicked Good Muffins Cookbook" is an experience. It's an invitation to explore the delectable world of muffins - a world where creativity reigns and where the simple act of baking can bring immense satisfaction and joy. This book will guide you to bake, taste, and share muffins of all shapes and sizes, flavors and textures, and sweet and savory notes. It's about more than just filling your home with the heavenly scent of freshly baked muffins. It's about the smiles that come after the first bite, the laughter shared in the kitchen, and the memories made while enjoying these homemade treats.

As you delve into this book, we hope you discover new favorites and revisit beloved classics. We've tried to cover a wide spectrum of flavors and tastes, ensuring that every muffin lover, regardless of their preference, finds something to enjoy. Don't be afraid to take some creative liberties with these recipes - make them your own. Add a dash of your favorite spice, throw in some extra chocolate chips, or top with a crunchy streusel; the sky's the limit when it comes to customizing these recipes.

"The Quick and Easy Wicked Good Muffins Cookbook" is also a testament to the adage "good things come in small packages". Despite their size, muffins pack a punch in terms of flavor and satisfaction. They're a symbol of homely comfort and culinary creativity, a treat that's as enjoyable to make as they are to eat.

Lastly, remember that baking is as much about the process as it is about the outcome. So, don your aprons, preheat your ovens, gather your ingredients, and most importantly, have fun! We hope this book inspires you to venture into the heart-warming world of muffin baking, creating wickedly good muffins that delight your senses and fill your hearts.

Let's bake some muffins!

CONTENTS

LET'S BAKE SOME MUFFINS!

Are you craving something sweet and delicious or savory and heartwarming? I am sure that nobody can resist moist, delicious, and fluffy muffins. Muffins are made for quick breakfast, brunch, or just a snack during the day. There are many different flavor combinations and a ton of variations you can make to make a great muffin. Usually, we all know a couple of muffin recipes that we make them over and over again, in fact, there are many other flavors possibilities and this cookbook has over 101 recipes that you can try from classics sweet and savory to veggie-based and even gluten-free, if you are watching your carbs intake!

I love cooking, and it has been a passion of mine since I was a little girl. I remember growing up with my family and I was always inspired by my mother's recipes. I especially enjoyed baking bread, cakes, cupcakes, and muffins. Sometimes it's the most ordinary things that make the whole life so extraordinary. Recently, I just come up with the idea to make a foolproof collection of recipes that will be always by your hand when craving some moist, delicious, and flavorful muffins. After all, how many times you find yourself being amazed by the simplicity of flavors and foods? That's what home cooking is all about. My heart gets so much warmer when I see my family around the table enjoying home-cooked meals and gather with each other.

I decided to make a cookbook about muffins and present different varieties of flavors. They are all decadent, delicious, and presentative. What I know for sure is that muffins can be made out of anything. And I mean anything. During the years, when developing new recipes for muffins, I have to admit that I had so many failures and not-so-good food pairings. If you want to try other recipes than the traditional vanilla and chocolate flavors, I have included flavor combos that you have never imagined are good together like bacon and maple syrup. I mean, they are good in breakfast pancakes, but have you ever tried this flavor in a muffin recipe? For me, it was a discovery that marked my home cooking experience.

For years, muffins have been a culinary experience worth trying in the kitchen for everyone, and I can bet that one of the first recipes to anyone who started cooking is some sort of muffins. It's very popularized food nowadays but people make some 5-10 flavors over and over again. What I love about this muffin collection is that you will find over 101 different flavors and all of them are equally delicious. If you don't want to use vegetable oil or butter because you have cholesterol, you can use healthier oils good for your health. I have already mentioned that muffins are a very versatile food that can be made both sweet and savory. No matter what flavor you will choose, I am sure you will enjoy it the most because all of them are equally delicious. With the right combination of ingredients, muffins can make a great dessert or after-school snack.

After all, muffins are every child's dream after a wholesome lunch. I like mine muffins served with a lightly whisked whipped cream. Sometimes I dust them with powdered sugar, sometimes I infuse the whipped cream with maple syrup, coffee, or honey depending on the muffin flavor I am consuming at the moment.

One of the main things that people always go back to muffins when they crave something sweet is the simplicity of making. Basically, all you need is a muffin pan, muffin liners, bowl, wire whisk, and spoon or ice cream scoop to transfer the batter equally into the muffin liners. Making the batter will take you no more than 5-10 minutes depending on the recipe, but it usually takes just 5 minutes. It's very important to combine the dry and then mix the wet ingredients separately.

If you don't want to mess with another bowl, it's better to mix the dry ingredients in the bowl first and then add all of the wet ingredients whisking them all the way through the dry ones. This will allow you to have moist, fluffy, and puffed muffins. Another thing to mention is that you need to be careful not to overmix the batter. Overmixed batter tends to have tough muffins, and that is something you don't want to taste and see after the baking time. I always say it's better to undermix and to have a little clump here and there than to overmix it. I have mentioned it in each recipe, so you will be all set up when making this delicious treat.

Another thing to mention is that all the additions like chopped nuts, dried cranberries, chocolate chips, raisins, other dried fruits are always best to add them just right before distributing the batter in the muffin liners.

I am sure that no matter, what type of flavor you will choose, you will enjoy the texture, flavor, and the whole process of making muffins. It will take 5 minutes of making the muffin batter and another 15-20 minutes of baking them in the over. Making good muffins requires quality ingredients, gather them together properly, and then mixing them and folding them together for successful baking. For good muffins, you will need foolproof recipes, and I have collected them and pack them all together in this cookbook for your baking success. Spending time in the kitchen is never wasted time. Grab a bowl, a whisk, and a muffin pan and with this book, you are on a good way to cook up a muffin storm!

CLASSIC FLAVORS

Vanilla Muffins

Makes 12 | Prep time 10 minutes | Cooking time 15 minutes

Ingredients

1 ½ cups all-purpose flour
1 cup granulated sugar
1 teaspoon baking powder
¾ cup vegetable oil
1 large egg, room temperature
3 teaspoons vanilla extract
1 cup whole milk
Cooking spray or vegetable oil for greasing (optional)

Directions

1. Preheat the oven to 350°F (177°C).
2. Line a muffin pan with muffin liners or grease each hole with cooking spray or vegetable oil.
3. In a mixing bowl, mix the flour and baking powder.
4. In another large bowl, whisk the vegetable oil, egg, sugar, vanilla, and milk.
5. Add the dry ingredients to the wet ingredients and mix until combined. Be careful not to overmix the batter.
6. Transfer the batter to the muffin pan, filling the liners just ¾ full to allow room for the muffins to rise.
7. Bake in the oven for about 12–15 minutes or until a toothpick inserted in the center comes out clean.
8. Remove from the oven and let the muffins rest in the pan for 5 minutes. Then, transfer to a wire rack to cool down.
9. Serve and enjoy.

Nutrition (per serving)
Calories 261, fat 14.9 g, carbs 29.9 g
Protein 2.8 g, sodium 15 mg

Chocolate Muffins

Makes 12 | Prep time 10 minutes | Cooking time 15 minutes

Ingredients
¾ cup all-purpose flour
½ cup cocoa powder
1 cup sugar
¾ teaspoon baking powder
½ teaspoon baking soda
⅓ cup vegetable oil
2 large eggs, room temperature
2 teaspoons vanilla extract
½ cup whole milk
Cooking spray or vegetable oil for greasing (optional)

Directions

1. Preheat the oven to 350°F (177°C).
2. Line a muffin pan with muffin liners or grease each hole with cooking spray or vegetable oil.
3. In a mixing bowl, mix the flour, cocoa powder, baking powder, and baking soda.
4. In another large bowl, whisk the vegetable oil with the sugar and eggs.
5. Add the dry ingredients to the wet ingredients and mix until combined.
6. Transfer the batter to the muffin pan, filling the liners just ¾ full to allow room for the muffins to rise.
7. Bake in the oven for about 12–15 minutes or until a toothpick inserted in the center comes out clean.
8. Remove from the oven and let the muffins rest in the pan for 5 minutes. Then, transfer to a wire rack to cool down.
9. Serve and enjoy.

Nutrition (per serving)
Calories 173, fat 7.8 g, carbs 25.4 g,
Protein 2.8 g, sodium 69 mg

Chocolate Chip Muffins

Makes 12 I Prep time 10 minutes I Cooking time 15 minutes

Ingredients
1 ½ cups all-purpose flour
1 cup granulated sugar
1 teaspoon baking powder
¾ cup vegetable oil
1 large egg, room temperature
3 teaspoons vanilla extract
1 cup whole milk
½ cup semi-sweet chocolate chips
Cooking spray or vegetable oil for greasing (optional)

Directions

1. Preheat the oven at 350°F (177°C).
2. Line a muffin pan with muffin liners or grease each hole with cooking spray or vegetable oil.
3. In a mixing bowl, mix the flour, and baking powder.
4. In another large bowl, whisk the vegetable oil, the egg, granulated sugar, vanilla extract, and whole milk.
5. Add the dry ingredients to the wet ingredients except for the chocolate chips and mix until combined. Be careful not to overmix the batter.
6. Stir in the chocolate chips.
7. Transfer the batter to the muffin pan, filling the liners just ¾ full to allow room for the muffins to rise.
8. Bake in the oven for about 12-15 minutes or until a toothpick inserted in the center comes out clean.
9. Remove from the oven and let the muffins rest in the pan for 5 minutes. Then, transfer to a wire rack to cool down.
10. Serve and enjoy.

Nutrition (per serving)
Calories 308, fat 17.6 g, carbs 35.9 g,
Protein 2.8 g, sodium 15 mg

Caramel Muffins

Makes 12 | Prep time 10 minutes | Cooking time 15 minutes

Ingredients
1 ½ cups all-purpose flour
¼ cup granulated sugar
¾ cup light brown sugar
1 teaspoon baking powder
½ teaspoon salt
½ teaspoon ground cinnamon
½ cup butter, softened
¾ cup sour cream
2 large eggs, room temperature
2 teaspoons vanilla extract
½ cup caramel sauce, soften and runny
Cooking spray or vegetable oil for greasing (optional)

Directions

1. Preheat the oven at 350°F (177°C).
2. Line a muffin pan with muffin liners or grease each hole with cooking spray or vegetable oil.
3. In a mixing bowl, mix the flour, baking powder, ground cinnamon, and salt.
4. In another large bowl, beat the butter with the granulated sugar and light brown sugar.
5. Pour in the sour cream and caramel sauce.
6. Add the dry ingredients to the wet ingredients and mix until combined. Be careful not to overmix the batter.
7. Transfer the batter to the muffin pan, filling the liners just ¾ full to allow room for the muffins to rise.
8. Bake in the oven for about 15-17 minutes or until a toothpick inserted in the center comes out clean.

9. Remove from the oven and let the muffins rest in the pan for 5 minutes. Then, transfer to a wire rack to cool down.
10. Serve and enjoy.

Nutrition (per serving)
Calories 255, fat 11.7 g, carbs 35.1 g,
Protein 3.4 g, sodium 222 mg

Cheesecake Muffins

Makes 14 | Prep time 10 minutes | Cooking time 30 minutes

Ingredients

For the crust

1 ½ cups graham cracker crumbs
¼ cup butter, melted
1 tablespoon granulated sugar

For the cheesecake

16 ounces cream cheese, softened
1 cup icing sugar
1 cup sour cream
2 large eggs, room temperature
2 teaspoons lemon juice
1 teaspoon vanilla extract
1 teaspoon cornstarch
Cooking spray or vegetable oil for greasing (optional)

Directions

1. Preheat the oven at 350°F (177°C).
2. Line a muffin pan with muffin liners or grease each hole with cooking spray or vegetable oil.
3. To make the crust in a mixing bowl, combine the graham cracker crumbs, granulated sugar with melted butter.
4. Transfer one tablespoon full into a muffin pan lined with muffin liners. Tap them to spread the graham cracker crumbs evenly.
5. To make the cream cheese filling, in a mixing bowl, combine the cream cheese, icing sugar, eggs, sour cream, lemon juice, vanilla extract, and cornstarch.
6. Transfer the batter to the muffin pan, filling the liners just ¾ full to allow room for the muffins to rise.

7. Bake in the oven for about 30 minutes or until the middle part of the cheesecake is set.
8. Remove from the oven and let the muffins rest in the pan for 5 minutes. Then, transfer to a wire rack to cool down.
9. Serve and enjoy.

Nutrition (per serving)
Calories 248, fat 18.3 g, carbs 17.4 g,
Protein 4.2 g, sodium 204 mg

Sweet Corn Muffins

Makes 12 | Prep time 10 minutes | Cooking time 15 minutes

Ingredients

1 ¼ cups all-purpose flour
¾ cup cornmeal
¼ cup granulated sugar
1 ½ teaspoon baking powder
⅓ cup vegetable oil
2 large eggs, room temperature
2 teaspoons vanilla extract
2 tablespoons honey
¾ cup whole milk
Cooking spray or vegetable oil for greasing (optional)

Directions

1. Preheat the oven at 350°F (177°C).
2. Line a muffin pan with muffin liners or grease each hole with cooking spray or vegetable oil.
3. In a mixing bowl, mix the flour, cornmeal, and baking powder.
4. In another large bowl, with the help of a spatula, mix in the oil, honey, and granulated sugar until combined.
5. Stir in the eggs.
6. Add the dry ingredients to the wet ingredients and mix until combined. Be careful not to overmix the batter.
7. Stir in the vanilla extract.
8. Transfer the batter to the muffin pan, filling the liners just ¾ full to allow room for the muffins to rise.
9. Bake in the oven for about 12-15 minutes or until a toothpick inserted in the center comes out clean.

10. Remove from the oven and let the muffins rest in the pan for 5 minutes. Then, transfer to a wire rack to cool down.
11. Serve and enjoy.

Nutrition (per serving)

Calories 179, fat 7.8 g, carbs 24 g,

Protein 3.5 g, sodium 21 mg

Walnut Muffins

Makes 12 | Prep time 10 minutes | Cooking time 15 minutes

Ingredients

1 cup all-purpose flour
½ cup ground walnuts
1 teaspoon baking powder
½ teaspoon baking soda
1 teaspoon ground cinnamon
Pinch of salt
½ cup butter, softened
½ cup light brown sugar
¼ cup granulated sugar
2 large eggs, room temperature
1 teaspoon vanilla extract
¾ cup whole milk
Cooking spray or vegetable oil for greasing (optional)

Directions

1. Preheat the oven at 350°F (177°C).
2. Line a muffin pan with muffin liners or grease each hole with cooking spray or vegetable oil.
3. In a mixing bowl, mix the flour, ground walnuts, baking soda, ground cinnamon, salt, and baking powder
4. In another large bowl, with the help of a spatula mix in the butter with the light brown sugar and granulated sugar.
5. Add the dry ingredients to the wet ingredients and mix until combined. It will be lumpy and clumpy but that's totally fine. Stir in the whole milk.
6. Stir in the vanilla extract.

7. Transfer the batter to the muffin pan, filling the liners just ¾ full to allow room for the muffins to rise.
8. Bake in the oven for about 12-15 minutes or until a toothpick inserted in the center comes out clean.
9. Remove from the oven and let the muffins rest in the pan for 5 minutes. Then, transfer to a wire rack to cool down.
10. Serve and enjoy.

Nutrition (per serving)
Calories 200, fat 12.2 g, carbs 19.7 g,
Protein 4 g, sodium 138 mg

Maple Muffins

Makes 12 I Prep time 10 minutes I Cooking time 15 minutes

Ingredients
1 ½ cup all-purpose flour
1 teaspoon baking powder
½ teaspoon baking soda
Pinch of salt
½ cup butter, softened
1 cup light brown sugar
2 large eggs, room temperature
1 teaspoon vanilla extract
⅓ cup maple syrup
⅓ cup whole milk
Cooking spray or vegetable oil for greasing (optional)

Directions

1. Preheat the oven at 350°F (177°C).
2. Line a muffin pan with muffin liners or grease each hole with cooking spray or vegetable oil.
3. In a mixing bowl, mix the flour, baking soda, salt, and baking powder
4. In another large bowl, with the help of a spatula mix in the butter with the light brown sugar.
5. Stir in the eggs and mix until combined. Stir in the whole milk and maple syrup.
6. Add the dry ingredients to the wet ingredients and mix until combined. Be careful not to overmix the batter.
7. Stir in the vanilla extract.
8. Transfer the batter to the muffin pan, filling the liners just ¾ full to allow room for the muffins to rise.

9. Bake in the oven for about 12-15 minutes or until a toothpick inserted in the center comes out clean.
10. Remove from the oven and let the muffins rest in the pan for 5 minutes. Then, transfer to a wire rack to cool down.
11. Serve and enjoy.

Nutrition (per serving)
Calories 195, fat 8.2 g, carbs 27.9 g,
Protein 2.7 g, sodium 129 mg

Honey Buttermilk Muffins

Makes 12 | Prep time 10 minutes | Cooking time 15 minutes

Ingredients
1 ½ cup all-purpose flour
1 ½ teaspoon baking powder
Pinch of salt
½ cup butter, softened
1 cup light brown sugar
2 large eggs, room temperature
1 teaspoon vanilla extract
⅓ cup honey
⅓ cup buttermilk
Cooking spray or vegetable oil for greasing (optional)

Directions

1. Preheat the oven at 350°F (177°C).
2. Line a muffin pan with muffin liners or grease each hole with cooking spray or vegetable oil.
3. In a mixing bowl, mix the flour, salt, and baking powder
4. In another large bowl, with the help of a spatula, mix in the butter with the light brown sugar.
5. Stir in the eggs and mix until combined. Stir in the buttermilk and honey.
6. Add the dry ingredients to the wet ingredients and mix until combined. Be careful not to overmix the batter.
7. Stir in the vanilla extract.
8. Transfer the batter to the muffin pan, filling the liners just ¾ full to allow room for the muffins to rise.
9. Bake in the oven for about 12-15 minutes or until a toothpick inserted in the center comes out clean.

10. Remove from the oven and let the muffins rest in the pan for 5 minutes. Then, transfer to a wire rack to cool down.
11. Serve and enjoy.

Nutrition (per serving)
Calories 216, fat 8.7 g, carbs 32.3 g,
Protein 3 g, sodium 90 mg

Honey and Walnut Muffins

Makes 12 I Prep time 10 minutes I Cooking time 15 minutes

Ingredients
1 ½ cup all-purpose flour
1 ½ teaspoon baking powder
Pinch of salt
½ cup vegetable oil
1 cup light brown sugar
2 large eggs, room temperature
1 teaspoon vanilla extract
⅓ cup honey
⅓ cup whole milk
¾ cup walnuts, chopped
Cooking spray or vegetable oil for greasing (optional)

Directions

1. Preheat the oven at 350°F (177°C).
2. Line a muffin pan with muffin liners or grease each hole with cooking spray or vegetable oil.
3. In a mixing bowl, mix the flour, salt, and baking powder
4. In another large bowl, with the help of a spatula, mix in the butter with the light brown sugar.
5. Stir in the eggs and mix until combined. Stir in the whole milk and honey.
6. Add the dry ingredients to the wet ingredients and mix until combined. Be careful not to overmix the batter.
7. Stir in the vanilla extract and chopped walnuts.
8. Transfer the batter to the muffin pan, filling the liners just ¾ full to allow room for the muffins to rise.
9. Bake in the oven for about 12-15 minutes or until a toothpick inserted in the center comes out clean.

10. Remove from the oven and let the muffins rest in the pan for 5 minutes. Then, transfer to a wire rack to cool down.
11. Serve and enjoy.

Nutrition (per serving)
Calories 278, fat 14.9 g, carbs 33 g,
Protein 4.8g, sodium 31 mg

Almond Muffins

Makes 12 | Prep time 10 minutes | Cooking time 15 minutes

Ingredients
¾ cup all-purpose flour
½ cup ground almonds
1 ½ teaspoon baking powder
Pinch of salt
¼ cup vegetable oil
½ cup water
1 cup granulated sugar
1 large egg, room temperature
1 teaspoon vanilla extract
1 ½ teaspoon almond extract
½ cup sour cream
Cooking spray or vegetable oil for greasing (optional)

Directions

1. Preheat the oven at 350°F (177°C).
2. Line a muffin pan with muffin liners or grease each hole with cooking spray or vegetable oil.
3. In a mixing bowl, mix the flour, ground almonds, salt, and baking powder
4. In another large bowl, with the help of a wire, whisk mix in the oil, water with the granulated sugar.
5. Stir in the egg and mix until combined. Then, stir in the sour cream.
6. Add the dry ingredients to the wet ingredients and mix until combined. Be careful not to overmix the batter.
7. Stir in the vanilla and almond extract.
8. Transfer the batter to the muffin pan, filling the liners just ¾ full to allow room for the muffins to rise.

9. Bake in the oven for about 12-15 minutes or until a toothpick inserted in the center comes out clean.
10. Remove from the oven and let the muffins rest in the pan for 5 minutes. Then, transfer to a wire rack to cool down.
11. Serve and enjoy.

Nutrition (per serving)
Calories 182, fat 9 g, carbs 24.3 g,
Protein 2.5 g, sodium 24 mg

Whole Wheat Bran Muffins

Makes 12 | Prep time 10 minutes | Cooking time 15–17 minutes

Ingredients

¼ cup oil
¼ cup sugar
¼ cup honey
2 eggs
1 cup milk
1 ½ cups wheat bran
1 cup whole wheat flour
1 ½ teaspoon baking powder
½ teaspoon baking soda
1 teaspoon salt
Cooking spray or vegetable oil for greasing (optional)

Directions

1. Preheat the oven to 400°F (204ºC). Line a muffin pan with muffin liners or grease each hole with cooking spray or vegetable oil.
2. In a mixing bowl, combine the oil, sugar, honey, eggs, and milk.
3. Add the bran and mix well.
4. In a separate bowl, mix the flour, baking powder, baking soda, and salt.
5. Add the dry ingredients to the wet ingredients, and mix to combine.
6. Transfer the batter to the muffin pan, filling the liners just ¾ full to allow room for the muffins to rise.

7. Bake in the oven for about 20 minutes or until a toothpick inserted in the center comes out clean.
8. Remove from the oven and let the muffins rest in the pan for 5 minutes. Then, transfer to a wire rack to cool down.

Nutrition (per serving)

Calories 148, fat 2.1 g, carbs 32.7 g,
Protein 4 g, sodium 153 mg

Coconut Muffins

Makes 12 | Prep time 10 minutes | Cooking time 15 minutes

Ingredients
1 ½ cups all-purpose flour
1 ½ teaspoons baking powder
½ teaspoon salt
1 ¼ cups coconut flakes
¾ cup butter, softened
1 cup granulated sugar
1 cup buttermilk
2 large eggs, room temperature
1 teaspoon vanilla extract
Cooking spray or vegetable oil for greasing (optional)

Directions

1. Preheat the oven at 350°F (177°C).
2. Line a muffin pan with muffin liners or grease each hole with cooking spray or vegetable oil.
3. In a mixing bowl, mix the flour, baking powder, coconut flakes, and salt.
4. In another large bowl, beat the butter with the granulated sugar.
5. Stir in the eggs, buttermilk, and mix until combined.
6. Stir in vanilla extract.
7. Add the dry ingredients to the wet ingredients and mix until combined. Be careful not to overmix the batter.
8. Transfer the batter to the muffin pan, filling the liners just ¾ full to allow room for the muffins to rise.
9. Bake in the oven for about 20 minutes or until a toothpick inserted in the center comes out clean.

10. Remove from the oven and let the muffins rest in the pan for 5 minutes. Then, transfer to a wire rack to cool down.
11. Serve and enjoy.

Nutrition (per serving)
Calories 268, fat 15 g, carbs 31.1 g,
Protein 3.7 g, sodium 214 mg

Coconut Chocolate Muffins

Makes 12 | Prep time 10 minutes | Cooking time 15 minutes

Ingredients
1 cup all-purpose flour
½ cup cocoa powder
1 ½ teaspoons baking powder
½ teaspoon salt
1 ¼ cups coconut flakes
¾ cup vegetable oil
1 cup granulated sugar
1 cup buttermilk
2 large eggs, room temperature
1 teaspoon vanilla extract
Cooking spray or vegetable oil for greasing (optional)

Directions

1. Preheat the oven at 350°F (177°C).
2. Line a muffin pan with muffin liners or grease each hole with cooking spray or vegetable oil.
3. In a mixing bowl, mix the flour, cocoa powder, baking powder, coconut flakes, and salt.
4. In another large bowl, whisk the vegetable oil and granulated sugar.
5. Stir in the eggs, buttermilk, and mix until combined.
6. Stir in vanilla extract.
7. Add the dry ingredients to the wet ingredients and mix until combined. Be careful not to overmix the batter.
8. Transfer the batter to the muffin pan, filling the liners just ¾ full to allow room for the muffins to rise.
9. Bake in the oven for about 20 minutes or until a toothpick inserted in the center comes out clean.

10. Remove from the oven and let the muffins rest in the pan for 5 minutes. Then, transfer to a wire rack to cool down.
11. Serve and enjoy.

Nutrition (per serving)
Calories 276, fat 17.6 g, carbs 29 g,
Protein 3.7 g, sodium 133 mg

Oatmeal Raisin Muffins

Makes 12 I Prep time 10 minutes I Cooking time 15 minutes

Ingredients
1 ½ cups all-purpose flour
1 cup old fashioned oats
1 ½ teaspoons baking powder
Pinch of salt
2 large eggs, room temperature
⅔ cup brown sugar
½ cup vegetable oil
½ cup whole milk
1 cup raisins
Cooking spray or vegetable oil for greasing (optional)

Directions

1. Preheat the oven at 350°F (177°C).
2. Line a muffin pan with muffin liners or grease each hole with cooking spray or vegetable oil.
3. In a mixing bowl, mix the flour, oats, salt, and baking powder.
4. In another large bowl, with the help of a spatula, mix in the vegetable oil, eggs, light brown sugar, whole milk.
5. Add the dry ingredients to the wet ingredients and mix until combined. Be careful not to overmix the batter.
6. Stir in the raisins.
7. Transfer the batter to the muffin pan, filling the liners just ¾ full to allow room for the muffins to rise.
8. Bake in the oven for about 12-15 minutes or until a toothpick inserted in the center comes out clean.
9. Remove from the oven and let the muffins rest in the pan for 5 minutes. Then, transfer to a wire rack to cool down.

10. Serve and enjoy.

Nutrition (per serving)
Calories 275, fat 11.3 g, carbs 39.2 g,
Protein 5 g, sodium 32 mg

Oatmeal Chocolate Chip Muffins

Makes 12 | Prep time 10 minutes | Cooking time 15 minutes

Ingredients
1 ½ cups all-purpose flour
1 cup old fashioned oats
1 ½ teaspoons baking powder
Pinch of salt
2 large eggs, room temperature
⅔ cup granulated sugar
½ cup vegetable oil
½ cup buttermilk
¾ cup chocolate chips
Cooking spray or vegetable oil for greasing (optional)

Directions

1. Preheat the oven at 350°F (177°C).
2. Line a muffin pan with muffin liners or grease each hole with cooking spray or vegetable oil.
3. In a mixing bowl, mix the flour, oats, salt, and baking powder.
4. In another large bowl, with the help of a spatula, mix in the vegetable oil, eggs, granulated sugar, and buttermilk.
5. Add the dry ingredients to the wet ingredients and mix until combined. Be careful not to overmix the batter.
6. Stir in the chocolate chips.
7. Transfer the batter to the muffin pan, filling the liners just ¾ full to allow room for the muffins to rise.
8. Bake in the oven for about 12-15 minutes or until a toothpick inserted in the center comes out clean.
9. Remove from the oven and let the muffins rest in the pan for 5 minutes. Then, transfer to a wire rack to cool down.

10. Serve and enjoy.

Nutrition (per serving)
Calories 304, fat 14.1 g, carbs 39.1 g,
Protein 5.5 g, sodium 43 mg

Classic Molasses Muffins

Makes 12 | Prep time 10 minutes | Cooking time 18–20 minutes

Ingredients
1 ¼ cups all-purpose flour
¼ cup sugar
½ teaspoon baking soda
½ teaspoon ground ginger
½ teaspoon cinnamon
¼ teaspoon nutmeg
¼ teaspoon salt
1 egg
½ cup water
¼ cup vegetable oil
¼ cup molasses
Cooking spray or vegetable oil for greasing (optional)

Directions

1. Preheat the oven to 350°F (177°C). Line a muffin pan with muffin liners or grease each hole with cooking spray or vegetable oil.
2. In a mixing bowl, combine the flour, sugar, baking soda, ginger, cinnamon, nutmeg, and salt.
3. In another large bowl, beat the egg with the water, oil, and molasses.
4. Add the dry ingredients to the wet ingredients and mix until combined.
5. Transfer the batter to the muffin pan, filling the liners just ¾ full to allow room for the muffins to rise.
6. Bake in the oven for about 12-15 minutes or until a toothpick inserted in the center comes out clean.

7. Remove from the oven and let the muffins rest in the pan for 5 minutes. Then, transfer to a wire rack to cool down.

Nutrition (per serving)
Calories 149, fat 3 g, carbs 29 g,
Protein 3.1 g, sodium 263 mg

FRUIT-BASED MUFFINS

Lemon Muffins

Makes 12 | Prep time 10 minutes | Cooking time 15 minutes

Ingredients

1 ½ cups all-purpose flour
1 cup granulated sugar
2 teaspoons baking powder
½ teaspoon salt
½ cup butter, softened
½ cup whole milk
2 large eggs, room temperature
2 teaspoons vanilla extract
zest of 1 lemon
⅓ cup lemon juice
Cooking spray or vegetable oil for greasing (optional)

Directions

1. Preheat the oven at 350°F (177°C).
2. Line a muffin pan with muffin liners or grease each hole with cooking spray or vegetable oil.
3. In a mixing bowl, mix the flour, baking powder, and salt.
4. In another large bowl, beat the butter with the granulated sugar.
5. Stir in the eggs, whole milk, lemon zest, and lemon juice and mix until combined.
6. Stir in vanilla extract.
7. Add the dry ingredients to the wet ingredients and mix until combined. Be careful not to overmix the batter.
8. Transfer the batter to the muffin pan, filling the liners just ¾ full to allow room for the muffins to rise.

9. Bake in the oven for about 12-15 minutes or until a toothpick inserted in the center comes out clean.
10. Remove from the oven and let the muffins rest in the pan for 5 minutes. Then, transfer to a wire rack to cool down.
11. Serve with a dusting of powder sugar and enjoy.

Nutrition (per serving)
Calories 210, fat 9 g, carbs 29.8 g,
Protein 3.1 g, sodium 170 mg

Blueberry Muffins

Makes 12 | Prep time 10 minutes | Cooking time 20 minutes

Ingredients
1 ½ cups all-purpose flour
1 cup granulated sugar
2 teaspoons baking powder
½ teaspoon salt
½ cup butter, softened
½ cup buttermilk
2 large eggs, room temperature
2 teaspoons vanilla extract
zest of 1 lemon
1 tablespoon lemon juice
1 cup fresh blueberries
Cooking spray or vegetable oil for greasing (optional)

Directions

1. Preheat the oven at 350°F (177°C).
2. Line a muffin pan with muffin liners or grease each hole with cooking spray or vegetable oil.
3. In a mixing bowl, mix the flour, baking powder, and salt.
4. In another large bowl, beat the butter with the granulated sugar.
5. Stir in the eggs, buttermilk, lemon zest, and lemon juice and mix until combined.
6. Stir in vanilla extract.
7. Add the dry ingredients to the wet ingredients and mix until combined. Be careful not to overmix the batter.
8. Fold the blueberries in the batter and mix gently.
9. Transfer the batter to the muffin pan, filling the liners just ¾ full to allow room for the muffins to rise.

10. Bake in the oven for about 18-20 minutes or until a toothpick inserted in the center comes out clean.
11. Remove from the oven and let the muffins rest in the pan for 5 minutes. Then, transfer to a wire rack to cool down.
12. Serve with your favorite lemonade recipe.

Nutrition (per serving)
Calories 213, fat 8.8 g, carbs 31.5 g,
Protein 3.2 g, sodium 175 mg

Blueberry Crunch Muffins

Makes 6 | Prep time 20–30 minutes | Cooking time 30 minutes

Ingredients
Topping
⅓ cup all-purpose flour
⅓ cup coarse or raw sugar
¼ cup unsalted cold butter, cut into four pieces

Muffins
¾ cup sugar
1½ cups all-purpose flour
2 teaspoons baking powder
⅓ cup vegetable oil
½ teaspoon salt
1 large egg
⅓ cup buttermilk
1 cup frozen wild blueberries
2 teaspoons vanilla extract
Cooking spray or vegetable oil for greasing (optional)

Directions

1. Preheat the oven to 400°F (204°C). Line a muffin pan with muffin liners or grease each hole with cooking spray or vegetable oil.
2. To make the topping, add the flour, sugar, and cold butter to a mixing bowl. Mix well to form crumbs.
3. To make the muffins, add the flour, sugar, baking powder, and salt to another mixing bowl. Mix well.
4. Add the oil and eggs; whisk to mix well. Add the buttermilk and vanilla; mix again. Add a little more buttermilk if desired.

5. Add the dry ingredients to the wet ingredients and mix until combined. Add the blueberries and mix again.
6. Transfer the batter to the muffin pan, filling the liners just ¾ full to allow room for the muffins to rise.
7. Bake in the oven for about 12-15 minutes or until a toothpick inserted in the center comes out clean.
8. Remove from the oven and let the muffins rest in the pan for 5 minutes. Then, transfer to a wire rack to cool down.
9. Let cool on a wire rack; serve warm.

Nutrition (per serving)

Calories 213, fat 8.8 g, carbs 31.5 g,
Protein 3.2 g, sodium 175 mg

Easy Cherry Muffins

Makes 12 | Prep time 10 minutes | Cooking time 18–20 minutes

Ingredients
1 ¼ cups flour
½ cup sugar
1 ½ teaspoons baking powder
¼ teaspoon salt
¼ cup cold butter
1 egg, lightly beaten
3 tablespoons milk
1 teaspoon vanilla
1 can cherry pie filling
Cooking spray or vegetable oil for greasing (optional)

For the topping
½ cup flour
¼ cup brown sugar
½ teaspoon cinnamon
¼ cup cold butter

Directions

1. Preheat the oven to 350°F (177°C). Line a muffin pan with muffin liners or grease each hole with cooking spray or vegetable oil.
2. Combine the flour, sugar, baking powder, and salt. Cut in the butter until coarse crumbs are formed.
3. In a separate bowl, combine the egg, milk, and vanilla. Beat them together and mix them into the dry ingredients.
4. Transfer the batter to the muffin pan, filling the liners just ¾ full to allow room for the muffins to rise. Place a spoonful of cherry pie filling on top.

5. Make the topping. Mix the flour, brown sugar, and cinnamon. Cut in the butter.
6. Sprinkle the topping over the pie filling.
7. Bake for 18–20 minutes or until a toothpick inserted in the center comes out clean.
8. Remove from the oven and let the muffins rest in the pan for 5 minutes. Then, transfer to a wire rack to cool down.

Nutrition (per serving)
Calories 271, fat 6.8 g, carbs 49 g,
Protein 3.6 g, sodium 146 mg

Cherry Chocolate Muffins

Makes 12 | Prep time 15 minutes | Cooking time 18–20 minutes

Ingredients
1 ½ cups fresh cherries
3 ounces semi-sweet chocolate
2 cups all-purpose flour
½ cup granulated sugar
2 teaspoons baking powder
¼ teaspoon salt
1 cup whole milk
½ cup vegetable oil
1 large egg
1 ½ teaspoons pure vanilla extract
Coarse sugar for dusting
Cooking spray or vegetable oil for greasing (optional)

Directions

1. Pit and cut the cherries into halves and set aside.
2. Chop coarsely the chocolate and set aside.
3. Preheat the oven to 350°F (177°C). Line a muffin pan with muffin liners or grease each hole with cooking spray or vegetable oil.
4. In a large bowl, add the flour, sugar, baking powder, and salt. Stir to combine.
5. In another large bowl, add the milk, vegetable oil, egg, and vanilla. Whisk until smooth.
6. Add the milk mixture to the flour mixture and whisk until well combined.
7. Add the cherries and chocolate to the batter and stir to combine.

8. Transfer the batter to the muffin pan, filling the liners just ¾ full to allow room for the muffins to rise.
9. Bake in the oven for about 17-18 minutes or until a toothpick inserted in the center comes out clean.
10. Let cool for a few minutes in the pan and transfer to a wired rack to cool completely.
11. Dust with coarse sugar and serve.

Nutrition (per serving)
Calories 282, fat 13.6 g, carbs 34.9 g,
Protein 5.4 g, sodium 166 mg

Pear Muffins

Makes 14 | Prep time 10 minutes | Cooking time 17-18 minutes

Ingredients
1 ½ cups all-purpose flour
1½ teaspoon baking powder
1 teaspoon ground cinnamon
Pinch of salt
½ cup vegetable oil
¾ cup light brown sugar
2 large eggs, room temperature
½ cup buttermilk
1 teaspoon vanilla extract
1 cup pear, chopped
Cooking spray or vegetable oil for greasing (optional)

Directions

1. Preheat the oven at 350°F (177°C).
2. Line a muffin pan with muffin liners or grease each hole with cooking spray or vegetable oil.
3. In a mixing bowl, mix the flour, baking powder, ground cinnamon, and salt.
4. In another large bowl, mix the vegetable oil with the light brown sugar until creamy and fluffy.
5. Stir in the eggs and mix vigorously.
6. Mix in the buttermilk and vanilla extract.
7. Add the dry ingredients and fold them together with the wet ingredients.
8. Fold in the diced pear.
9. Transfer the batter to the muffin pan, filling the liners just ¾ full to allow room for the muffins to rise.

10. Bake in the oven for about 12-15 minutes or until a toothpick inserted in the center comes out clean.
11. Remove from the oven and let the muffins rest in the pan for 5 minutes. Then, transfer to a wire rack to cool down.
12. Serve and enjoy with a sprinkle of powdered sugar if desired.

Nutrition (per serving)
Calories 199, fat 10.2 g, carbs 24.7 g,
Protein 3.1 g, sodium 39 mg

Ginger and Pear Muffins

Makes 14 I Prep time 10 minutes I Cooking time 17-18 minutes

Ingredients

1 ½ cups all-purpose flour
1½ teaspoon baking powder
1 teaspoon ground cinnamon
Pinch of salt
½ cup butter, melted
¾ cup light brown sugar
2 large eggs, room temperature
½ cup whole milk
1 teaspoon vanilla extract
1 cup pear, chopped
3 cm ginger, grated
Cooking spray or vegetable oil for greasing (optional)

Directions

1. Preheat the oven at 350°F (177°C).
2. Line a muffin pan with muffin liners or grease each hole with cooking spray or vegetable oil.
3. In a mixing bowl, mix the flour, baking powder, ground cinnamon, and salt.
4. In another large bowl, mix the melted butter with the light brown sugar until creamy and fluffy.
5. Stir in the eggs and mix vigorously.
6. Mix in the whole milk and vanilla extract.
7. Add the dry ingredients and fold them together with the wet ingredients.
8. Fold in the diced pear and grated ginger.
9. Transfer the batter to the muffin pan, filling the liners just ¾ full to allow room for the muffins to rise.

10. Bake in the oven for about 12-15 minutes or until a toothpick inserted in the center comes out clean.
11. Remove from the oven and let the muffins rest in the pan for 5 minutes. Then, transfer to a wire rack to cool down.
12. Serve and enjoy with a sprinkle of powdered sugar if desired.

Nutrition (per serving)
Calories 190, fat 9 g, carbs 25 g,

Protein 3.2 g, sodium 87 mg

Apple Muffins

Makes 14 | Prep time 10 minutes | Cooking time 17-18 minutes

Ingredients
1 ½ cups all-purpose flour
1½ teaspoon baking powder
1 teaspoon ground cinnamon
Pinch of salt
½ cup vegetable oil
¾ cup light brown sugar
2 large eggs, room temperature
½ cup whole milk
1 teaspoon vanilla extract
1 cup apple, chopped
Cooking spray or vegetable oil for greasing (optional)

Directions

1. Preheat the oven at 350°F (177°C).
2. Line a muffin pan with muffin liners or grease each hole with cooking spray or vegetable oil.
3. In a mixing bowl, mix the flour, baking powder, ground cinnamon, and salt.
4. In another large bowl, mix the vegetable oil with the light brown sugar until creamy and fluffy.
5. Stir in the eggs and mix vigorously.
6. Mix in the whole milk and vanilla extract.
7. Add the dry ingredients and fold them together with the wet ingredients.
8. Fold in the diced apple.
9. Transfer the batter to the muffin pan, filling the liners just ¾ full to allow room for the muffins to rise.

10. Bake in the oven for about 12-15 minutes or until a toothpick inserted in the center comes out clean.
11. Remove from the oven and let the muffins rest in the pan for 5 minutes. Then, transfer to a wire rack to cool down.
12. Serve and enjoy with a sprinkle of powdered sugar if desired.

Nutrition (per serving)
Calories 203, fat 10.4 g, carbs 25.2 g,

Protein 3.1 g, sodium 32 mg

Applesauce Muffins

Makes 14-16 | Prep time 10 minutes | Cooking time 20 minutes

Ingredients
1 ½ cups all-purpose flour
1½ teaspoon baking powder
1 teaspoon ground cinnamon
Pinch of salt
½ cup butter
¾ cup granulated sugar
2 large eggs, room temperature
1 teaspoon vanilla extract
1 cup apple sauce
Cooking spray or vegetable oil for greasing (optional)

Directions

1. Preheat the oven at 350°F (177°C).
2. Line a muffin pan with muffin liners or grease each hole with cooking spray or vegetable oil.
3. In a mixing bowl, mix the flour, baking powder, ground cinnamon, and salt.
4. In another large bowl, beat the butter with the granulated sugar until creamy and fluffy.
5. Stir in the eggs and mix vigorously.
6. Mix in the apple sauce and vanilla extract.
7. Add the dry ingredients and fold them together with the wet ingredients.
8. Transfer the batter to the muffin pan, filling the liners just ¾ full to allow room for the muffins to rise.
9. Bake in the oven for about 12-15 minutes or until a toothpick inserted in the center comes out clean.

10. Remove from the oven and let the muffins rest in the pan for 5 minutes. Then, transfer to a wire rack to cool down.
11. Serve and enjoy.

Nutrition (per serving)
Calories 191, fat 8.7 g, carbs 26.8 g,
Protein 2.8 g, sodium 80 mg

Classic Apple Cinnamon Muffins

Makes 12 | Prep time 10 minutes | Cooking time 20 minutes

Ingredients

1 egg, beaten
½ cup milk
3 tablespoons butter, melted
1 ¼ cups peeled cooking apples, cored and chopped
½ teaspoon salt
1 ⅛ cups self-rising flour (1 cup + 2 tablespoons)
½ cup sugar
1 teaspoon cinnamon
Dash of ground cloves
Sugar to dredge
Cooking spray or vegetable oil for greasing (optional)

Directions

1. Preheat the oven to 350ºF (177ºC). Line a muffin pan with muffin liners or grease each hole with cooking spray or vegetable oil.
2. Whisk the egg in a mixing bowl. Mix in the milk, butter, and apples.
3. In another mixing bowl, mix the salt, flour, sugar, and spices.
4. Combine the mixtures and mix well.
5. Grease muffin pans with butter or cooking oil.
6. Transfer the batter to the muffin pan, filling the liners just ¾ full to allow room for the muffins to rise.
7. Bake for about 18-20 minutes until the tops are browned and a toothpick inserted in the middle comes out clean.

8. Remove from the oven and let the muffins rest in the pan for 5 minutes. Then, transfer to a wire rack to cool down.
9. Dredge in sugar and serve warm.

Nutrition (per serving)
Calories 210, fat 8 g, carbs 33 g,
Protein 5 g, sodium 110 mg

Apple Crumble Muffins

Makes 12 I Prep time 10 minutes I Cooking time 20 minutes

Ingredients
1 ½ cups all-purpose flour
1½ teaspoon baking powder
1 teaspoon ground cinnamon
Pinch of salt
¾ cup vegetable oil
1 ½ cup granulated sugar
3 large eggs, room temperature
1 teaspoon vanilla extract
1 cup apple, chopped into small cubes
Cooking spray or vegetable oil for greasing (optional)

For the crumble topping
2 tablespoons butter, cold
1 tablespoon light brown sugar
3 tablespoons all-purpose flour
pinch of cinnamon

Directions

1. Preheat the oven at 350°F (177°C).
2. Line a muffin pan with muffin liners or grease each hole with cooking spray or vegetable oil.
3. In a mixing bowl, mix the flour, baking powder, ground cinnamon, and salt.
4. In another large bowl, mix the vegetable oil with the granulated sugar until combined.
5. Stir in the eggs and mix vigorously.
6. Mix in the vanilla extract.
7. Add the dry ingredients and fold them together with the wet ingredients.

8. Fold in the diced apple.
9. Transfer the batter to the muffin pan, filling the liners just ¾ full to allow room for the muffins to rise.
10. In a small bowl mix the flour, light brown sugar, flour, ground cinnamon, and butter.
11. Rub with your finger to make the crumble topping.
12. Top each muffin with that crumble.
13. Bake in the oven for about 15-20 minutes or until a toothpick inserted in the center comes out clean.
14. Remove from the oven and let the muffins rest in the pan for 5 minutes. Then, transfer to a wire rack to cool down.
15. Serve and enjoy.

Nutrition (per serving)
Calories 322 fat 17 g, carbs 41.6 g,
Protein 3.3 g, sodium 46 mg

Apple Walnut Crunch Muffins

Makes 16 | Prep time 20 minutes | Cooking time 20–25 minutes

Ingredients
Muffins
¾ cup sugar
1½ cups all-purpose flour
¼ teaspoon baking soda
¼ teaspoon salt
2 teaspoons baking powder
1 teaspoon ground cinnamon
⅛ teaspoon ground nutmeg
¼ teaspoon ground allspice
1¼ cups sour cream
½ cup butter, melted
2 eggs
1 cup tart apple, chopped
¼ cup walnuts, chopped
Cooking spray or vegetable oil for greasing (optional)

Topping
¼ cup all-purpose flour
3 tablespoons sugar
½ cup walnuts, chopped
⅛ teaspoon ground nutmeg
¼ teaspoon ground cinnamon
2 tablespoons cold butter

Directions

1. Preheat the oven to 375°F (190°C). Line a muffin pan with muffin liners or grease each hole with cooking spray or vegetable oil.

2. Add the flour, cinnamon, baking powder, sugar, nutmeg, allspice, salt, and baking soda to a mixing bowl. Mix well.
3. Add the eggs to another mixing bowl and beat them. Add the butter and cream. Mix well.
4. Combine the mixtures and mix well. Mix in the apples and walnuts.
5. Transfer the batter to the muffin pan, filling the liners just ¾ full to allow room for the muffins to rise.
6. Add the flour, sugar, walnuts, cinnamon, and nutmeg to a mixing bowl. Mix well. Keep adding butter pieces and mixing to form coarse crumbs.
7. Sprinkle ⅔ of the topping over the muffins; pour the remaining batter over them and then top with the remaining crumbs.
8. Bake for about 20–25 minutes until golden brown around edges and a toothpick comes out clean.
9. Remove from the oven and let the muffins rest in the pan for 5 minutes. Then, transfer to a wire rack to cool down.
10. Let cool on a wire rack; serve warm.

Nutrition (per serving)
Calories 438 fat 15.6 g, carbs 67.9 g,
Protein 7.5 g, sodium 507 mg

Oatmeal Fruity Muffins

Makes 8 | Prep time 10 minutes | Cooking time 20 minutes

Ingredients

Olive oil cooking spray
1 cup oat flour
1 cup old-fashioned rolled oats
¼ cup flaxseed meal
½ teaspoon ground ginger
1 ¼ cups unsweetened applesauce
½ cup pineapples, chopped
¼ cup walnuts, chopped
2 teaspoons unsweetened coconut flakes
2 teaspoons orange zest, grated
Cooking spray or vegetable oil for greasing (optional)

Directions

1. Preheat the oven to 350°F (177°C).
2. Line a muffin pan with muffin liners or grease each hole with cooking spray or vegetable oil.
3. Add the oat flour, oats, flaxseed meal, and ginger to a large mixing bowl and mix well.
4. Add the applesauce and mix well.
5. Add the remaining ingredients and stir gently to combine.
6. Transfer the batter to the muffin pan, filling the liners just ¾ full to allow room for the muffins to rise.
7. Bake for approximately 20 minutes or until a toothpick inserted in the center comes out clean.
8. Place the muffin pan on a wire rack to cool for about 10 minutes.
9. Carefully invert the muffins onto the wire rack and let cool completely before serving.

Nutrition (per serving)
Calories 361, fat 10.4 g, carbs 59.7 g,
Protein 9.2 g, sodium 6 mg

Orange **Muffins**

Makes 12 | Prep time 10 minutes | Cooking time 15 minutes

Ingredients
1 cup all-purpose flour
½ cup ground almonds
1 ½ teaspoon baking powder
Pinch of salt
½ cup butter, softened
⅔ cup granulated sugar
⅓ cup orange juice
Zest of 1 orange
3 large eggs, room temperature
1 teaspoon vanilla extract
¾ cup whole milk
Cooking spray or vegetable oil for greasing (optional)

Directions

1. Preheat the oven at 350°F (177°C).
2. Line a muffin pan with muffin liners or grease each hole with cooking spray or vegetable oil.
3. In a mixing bowl, mix the flour, ground almonds, salt, and baking powder
4. In another large bowl, with the help of a wire whisk mix in the butter, and the granulated sugar. Fold in the orange juice.
5. Stir in the eggs and mix until combined. Then, stir in the whole milk.
6. Add the dry ingredients to the wet ingredients and mix until combined. Be careful not to overmix the batter.
7. Stir in the vanilla extract.

8.   Transfer the batter to the muffin pan, filling the liners just ¾ full to allow room for the muffins to rise.
9.   Bake in the oven for about 12-15 minutes or until a toothpick inserted in the center comes out clean.
10. Remove from the oven and let the muffins rest in the pan for 5 minutes. Then, transfer to a wire rack to cool down.
11. Serve and enjoy.

Nutrition (per serving)
Calories 203, fat 11.5 g, carbs 21.9 g,
Protein 4.1 g, sodium 91 mg

Orange Raisin Muffins

Makes 12 | Prep time 10 minutes | Cooking time 20 minutes

Ingredients

2 cups sifted all-purpose flour
¾ teaspoon baking soda
½ teaspoon salt
⅓ cup sugar
½ cup raisins
1 egg, beaten
⅓ cup orange juice
1 teaspoon grated orange rind
⅔ cup buttermilk
⅓ cup shortening, melted
Cooking spray or vegetable oil for greasing (optional)

Directions

1. Preheat the oven to 425°F (218°C) and prepare a muffin pan with butter or cooking spray.
2. Combine the flour, baking soda, salt, sugar, and raisins. Mix well, and set aside.
3. In a separate bowl, combine the egg, orange juice, orange rind, buttermilk, and melted shortening.
4. Add the dry ingredients to the wet ingredients and mix until combined.
5. Transfer the batter to the muffin pan, filling the liners just ¾ full to allow room for the muffins to rise.
6. Bake for 20 minutes or until a toothpick inserted in the center comes out clean.
7. Remove from the oven and let the muffins rest in the pan for 5 minutes. Then, transfer to a wire rack to cool down.

Nutrition (per serving)
Calories 206 fat 8 g, carbs 41.6 g,
Protein 3 g, sodium 419 mg

Almond Orange Muffins

Makes 6 | Prep time 10 minutes | Cooking time 30 minutes

Ingredients
2 tablespoons vegetable oil
¼ cup fresh orange juice
2 cups all-purpose flour, blanched
3 large eggs
½ teaspoon cardamom
1 teaspoon baking powder
¼ teaspoon sea salt
1 tablespoon orange zest
¼ cup white sugar
Cooking spray or vegetable oil for greasing (optional)

Directions

1. Preheat the oven to 350°F (175°C). Line a muffin pan with muffin liners or grease each hole with cooking spray or vegetable oil.
2. Whisk the eggs in a bowl. Add the orange juice and orange zest. Mix well.
3. Add the baking powder, cardamom, all-purpose flour, sugar, and salt to a mixing bowl. Mix well.
4. Add the dry ingredients to the wet ingredients and mix until combined.
5. Add the oil.
6. Mix well until no visible lumps remain.
7. Transfer the batter to the muffin pan, filling the liners just ¾ full to allow room for the muffins to rise.
8. Bake for 20 minutes or until a toothpick inserted in the center comes out clean.
9. Let cool inside the oven for 5 minutes.

10. Remove from oven and let muffins cool on a wire rack for about 10 minutes.
11. Gently remove muffins from cups and serve.

Nutrition (per serving)
Calories 257, fat 26 g, carbs 11 g,
Protein 12.5 g, sodium 218 mg

Pineapple Upside-Down Muffins

Makes 18 | Prep time 10 minutes | Cooking time 15 minutes

Ingredients

1 ½ cups all-purpose flour
1 ½ teaspoons baking powder
½ teaspoon salt
1 cup vegetable oil
1 cup granulated sugar
¼ cup whole milk
3 large egg whites, room temperature
1 teaspoon vanilla extract
20 ounces can pineapple chunks
½ cup butter, melted
1 ½ cups light brown sugar
Cooking spray or vegetable oil for greasing (optional)

Directions

1. Preheat the oven at 350°F (177°C).
2. Line a muffin pan with muffin liners or grease each hole with cooking spray or vegetable oil.
3. Place 1 teaspoon of melted butter in each muffin cup and spoon 1 tablespoon of light brown sugar. Place a heaping tablespoon of crushed pineapple over the light brown sugar.
4. In a mixing bowl, mix the flour, baking powder, and salt.
5. In another large bowl, beat the butter with the granulated sugar, whole milk eggs, and vanilla extract.
6. Add the dry ingredients to the wet ingredients and mix until combined.
7. Transfer the batter to the muffin pan, filling the liners just ¾ full to allow room for the muffins to rise.

8. Bake in the oven for about 20 minutes or until a toothpick inserted in the center comes out clean.
9. Remove from the oven and let the muffins rest in the pan for 5 minutes. Then, transfer to a wire rack to cool down.
10. Serve and enjoy.

Nutrition (per serving)

Calories 454, fat 26.2 g, carbs 54 g,

Protein 2.8 g, sodium 168 mg

Cranberry Muffins

Makes 16 I Prep time 10 minutes I Cooking time 15 minutes

Ingredients
1 ⅔ cups all-purpose flour
½ cup granulated sugar
½ cup light brown sugar
1 teaspoon baking powder
¾ cup vegetable oil
3 large eggs, room temperature
2 teaspoons vanilla extract
1 cup whole milk
1 cup dried cranberries
Cooking spray or vegetable oil for greasing (optional)

Directions

1. Preheat the oven at 350°F (177°C).
2. Line a muffin pan with muffin liners or grease each hole with cooking spray or vegetable oil.
3. In a mixing bowl, mix the flour and baking powder.
4. In another large bowl, whisk the vegetable oil and granulated sugar with the light brown sugar until combined.
5. Stir in the eggs, one at a time, mixing well between each addition.
6. Then alternatively add the whole milk with the dry ingredients and mix until combined. Be careful not to overmix the batter.
7. Stir in the vanilla extract and fold in the dried cranberries.
8. Transfer the batter to the muffin pan, filling the liners just ¾ full to allow room for the muffins to rise.

9. Bake in the oven for about 12-15 minutes or until a toothpick inserted in the center comes out clean.
10. Remove from the oven and let the muffins rest in the pan for 5 minutes. Then, transfer to a wire rack to cool down.
11. Serve and enjoy.

Nutrition (per serving)
Calories 275, fat 15.7 g, carbs 29.6 g,
Protein 4 g, sodium 28 mg

Cranberry Orange Muffins

Makes 6 | Prep time 25 minutes | Cooking time 30 minutes

Ingredients

1 tablespoon cornstarch
1½ cups all-purpose flour
1½ teaspoons baking powder
½ teaspoon baking soda
½ teaspoon salt
⅔ cup sugar
½ cup vegetable oil
½ cup buttermilk
2 large eggs
1 teaspoon vanilla extract
1½ cups fresh cranberries
2 teaspoons fresh orange zest
2 tablespoons turbinado sugar
Cooking spray or vegetable oil for greasing (optional)

Directions

1. Preheat the oven to 375°F (190°C). Line a muffin pan with muffin liners or grease each hole with cooking spray or vegetable oil.
2. Add the flour, cornstarch, baking powder, baking soda, and salt to a mixing bowl. Mix well.
3. Combine the sugar and oil in a large bowl. Add the eggs one by one and whisk well.
4. Mix in the vanilla.
5. Add the flour mixture and buttermilk to the egg mixture in batches, mixing after each addition to make a smooth batter.

6. Mix in the orange zest and 1 cup of cranberries.
7. Transfer the batter to the muffin pan, filling the liners just ¾ full to allow room for the muffins to rise. Add the remaining cranberries and turbinado sugar over the muffins.
8. Bake for about 25–30 minutes until golden brown around edges and a toothpick comes out clean.
9. Remove from the oven and let the muffins rest in the pan for 5 minutes. Then, transfer to a wire rack to cool down.
10. Serve warm.

Nutrition (per serving)
Calories 278 fat 9 g, carbs 46 g,
Protein 4 g, sodium 117 mg

Banana Cranberry Bran Muffins

Makes 18 | Prep time 15 minutes I Cooking time 25 minutes

Ingredients
2 ripe bananas, mashed
1 large egg
¼ cup coconut oil
⅓ cup milk
⅓ cup sugar
1 cup whole wheat flour
1 ¾ cups rolled oats
3 teaspoons baking powder
¼ cup walnuts, chopped
1-1½ cups fresh cranberries
Cinnamon
Cooking spray or vegetable oil for greasing (optional)

Preparation

1. Heat the oven to 375°F (190°C).
2. Line a muffin pan with muffin liners or grease each hole with cooking spray or vegetable oil.
3. Mash the bananas well before combining them with the egg, coconut oil, and milk.
4. Add the sugar, flour, rolled oats, baking powder, and a pinch of cinnamon. Mix just until incorporated. Gently fold in the walnuts and cranberries.
5. Transfer the batter to the muffin pan, filling the liners just ¾ full to allow room for the muffins to rise.
6. Bake for 20-25 minutes, or until a toothpick inserted in the center comes out clean.
7. Take the muffins out of the pan and cool on a wire rack.

Nutrition (per serving)

Calories 187, fats 6 g, carbs 29 g
Protein 5 g, sodium 12 mg

Banana Muffins

Makes 12 I Prep time 10 minutes I Cooking time 15 minutes

Ingredients
1 ½ cups all-purpose flour
1 cup light brown sugar
1 teaspoon baking powder
1 teaspoon ground cinnamon
½ cup vegetable oil
1 large egg, room temperature
2 large bananas, mashed
1 teaspoon vanilla extract
¼ cup whole milk
Cooking spray or vegetable oil for greasing (optional)

Directions

1. Preheat the oven at 350°F (177°C).
2. Line a muffin pan with muffin liners or grease each hole with cooking spray or vegetable oil.
3. In a mixing bowl, mix the flour, cinnamon, and baking powder.
4. In another whisk the vegetable oil and light brown sugar until combined.
5. Stir in the eggs. Stir in the mashed bananas.
6. Then alternatively add the whole milk with the dry ingredients and mix until combined. Be careful not to overmix the batter.
7. Stir in the vanilla extract.
8. Transfer the batter to the muffin pan, filling the liners just ¾ full to allow room for the muffins to rise.
9. Bake in the oven for about 12-15 minutes or until a toothpick inserted in the center comes out clean.

10. Remove from the oven and let the muffins rest in the pan for 5 minutes. Then, transfer to a wire rack to cool down.
11. Serve and enjoy.

Nutrition (per serving)
Calories 214, fat 9.9 g, carbs 29.6 g,
Protein 2.6 g, sodium 12 mg

Banana Macadamia Muffins

Makes 12 | Prep time 10 minutes | Cooking time 15 minutes

Ingredients
1 ½ cups all-purpose flour
1 cup light brown sugar
1 teaspoon baking powder
1 teaspoon ground cinnamon
½ cup vegetable oil
1 large egg, room temperature
2 large bananas, mashed
1 teaspoon vanilla extract
¼ cup buttermilk
¾ cup macadamia nuts, crushed
Cooking spray or vegetable oil for greasing (optional)

Directions

1. Preheat the oven at 350°F (177°C).
2. Line a muffin pan with muffin liners or grease each hole with cooking spray or vegetable oil.
3. In a mixing bowl, mix the flour, cinnamon, and baking powder.
4. In another whisk the vegetable oil and light brown sugar until combined.
5. Stir in the eggs. Stir in the mashed bananas.
6. Then alternatively add the buttermilk with the dry ingredients and mix until combined. Be careful not to overmix the batter.
7. Stir in the vanilla extract.
8. Transfer the batter to the muffin pan, filling the liners just ¾ full to allow room for the muffins to rise.
9. Top each muffin with crushed macadamia nuts.

10. Bake in the oven for about 12-15 minutes or until a toothpick inserted in the center comes out clean.
11. Remove from the oven and let the muffins rest in the pan for 5 minutes. Then, transfer to a wire rack to cool down.
12. Serve and enjoy.

Nutrition (per serving)
Calories 273, fat 16.1 g, carbs 30.8 g,

Protein 3.2 g, sodium 16 mg

Cranberry Walnut Muffins

Makes 16 I Prep time 10 minutes I Cooking time 15 minutes

Ingredients
1 ⅔ cups all-purpose flour
½ cup granulated sugar
½ cup light brown sugar
1 teaspoon baking powder
¾ cup vegetable oil
3 large eggs, room temperature
2 teaspoons vanilla extract
1 cup whole milk
1 cup dried cranberries
1 cup walnuts, chopped
Cooking spray or vegetable oil for greasing (optional)

Directions

1. Preheat the oven at 350°F (177°C).
2. Line a muffin pan with muffin liners or grease each hole with cooking spray or vegetable oil.
3. In a mixing bowl, mix the flour and baking powder.
4. In another large bowl, whisk the vegetable oil and granulated sugar with the light brown sugar until combined.
5. Stir in the eggs, one at a time, mixing well between each addition.
6. Then alternatively add the whole milk with the dry ingredients and mix until combined. Be careful not to overmix the batter.
7. Stir in the vanilla extract and fold in the dried cranberries and chopped walnuts.

8. Transfer the batter to the muffin pan, filling the liners just ¾ full to allow room for the muffins to rise.
9. Bake in the oven for about 12-15 minutes or until a toothpick inserted in the center comes out clean.
10. Remove from the oven and let the muffins rest in the pan for 5 minutes. Then, transfer to a wire rack to cool down.
11. Serve and enjoy.

Nutrition (per serving)
Calories 340, fat 21.9 g, carbs 30.7 g,
Protein 6.5 g, sodium 28 mg

Lemon Muffins

Makes 12 I Prep time 10 minutes I Cooking time 15 minutes

Ingredients
1 ½ cup all-purpose flour
1 ½ teaspoon baking powder
Pinch of salt
½ cup vegetable oil
⅔ cup granulated sugar
⅓ cup lemon juice
Zest of 1 lemon
3 large eggs, room temperature
1 teaspoon vanilla extract
¾ cup whole milk
Cooking spray or vegetable oil for greasing (optional)

Directions

1. Preheat the oven at 350°F (177°C).
2. Line a muffin pan with muffin liners or grease each hole with cooking spray or vegetable oil.
3. In a mixing bowl, mix the flour, salt, and baking powder
4. In another large bowl, with the help of a wire whisk mix in the vegetable oil, and the granulated sugar. Fold in the lemon juice and lemon zest.
5. Stir in the eggs and mix until combined. Then, stir in the whole milk.
6. Then add the dry ingredients and mix until combined. Be careful not to overmix the batter.
7. Stir in the vanilla extract.
8. Transfer the batter to the muffin pan, filling the liners just ¾ full to allow room for the muffins to rise.

9. Bake in the oven for about 12-15 minutes or until a toothpick inserted in the center comes out clean.
10. Remove from the oven and let the muffins rest in the pan for 5 minutes. Then, transfer to a wire rack to cool down.
11. Serve and enjoy.

Nutrition (per serving)
Calories 209, fat 11 g, carbs 24.3 g,
Protein 3.7 g, sodium 38 mg

Lemon Poppy Seed Muffins

Makes 12 I Prep time 10 minutes I Cooking time 15 minutes

Ingredients
1 ½ cup all-purpose flour
1 ½ teaspoon baking powder
Pinch of salt
½ cup vegetable oil
⅔ cup granulated sugar
⅓ cup lemon juice
zest of 1 lemon
3 large eggs, room temperature
1 teaspoon vanilla extract
¾ cup whole milk
½ cup poppy seeds
Cooking spray or vegetable oil for greasing (optional)

Directions

1. Preheat the oven at 350°F (177°C).
2. Line a muffin pan with muffin liners or grease each hole with cooking spray or vegetable oil.
3. In a mixing bowl, mix the flour, salt, and baking powder
4. In another large bowl, with the help of a wire whisk mix in the vegetable oil, and the granulated sugar. Fold in the lemon juice and lemon zest.
5. Stir in the eggs and mix until combined. Then, stir in the whole milk.
6. Then add the dry ingredients and mix until combined. Be careful not to overmix the batter. Stir in the vanilla extract and poppy seeds.
7. Transfer the batter to the muffin pan, filling the liners just ¾ full to allow room for the muffins to rise.

8. Bake in the oven for about 12-15 minutes or until a toothpick inserted in the center comes out clean.
9. Remove from the oven and let the muffins rest in the pan for 5 minutes. Then, transfer to a wire rack to cool down.
10. Serve and enjoy.

Nutrition (per serving)

Calories 239, fat 13.5 g, carbs 25.6 g,

Protein 4.7 g, sodium 39 mg

Lemon Crumb Muffins

Makes 12 I Prep time 10 minutes I Cooking time 15 minutes

Ingredients
1 ½ cup all-purpose flour
1 ½ teaspoon baking powder
Pinch of salt
½ cup vegetable oil
⅔ cup granulated sugar
⅓ cup lemon juice
zest of ½ lemon
3 large eggs, room temperature
1 teaspoon vanilla extract
¾ cup buttermilk
Cooking spray or vegetable oil for greasing (optional)

For the crumble topping
2 tablespoons butter, cold
1 tablespoon light brown sugar
3 tablespoons all-purpose flour
Zest of ½ lemon

Directions

1. Preheat the oven at 350°F (177°C).
2. Line a muffin pan with muffin liners or grease each hole with cooking spray or vegetable oil.
3. In a mixing bowl, mix the flour, salt, and baking powder
4. In another large bowl, with the help of a wire whisk mix in the vegetable oil, and the granulated sugar. Fold in the lemon juice and lemon zest.
5. Stir in the eggs and mix until combined. Then, stir in the whole milk.

6. Then add the dry ingredients and mix until combined. Be careful not to overmix the batter. Stir in the vanilla extract.
7. Transfer the batter to the muffin pan, filling the liners just ¾ full to allow room for the muffins to rise.
8. In a small bowl mix the flour, light brown sugar, flour, lemon zest, and butter.
9. Rub with your finger to make the crumble topping and top each muffin with the crumble.
10. Bake in the oven for about 12-15 minutes or until a toothpick inserted in the center comes out clean.
11. Remove from the oven and let the muffins rest in the pan for 5 minutes. Then, transfer to a wire rack to cool down.
12. Serve and enjoy.

Nutrition (per serving)
Calories 226, fat 12.6 g, carbs 25.1 g,
Protein 3.8 g, sodium 61 mg

Raspberry Muffins

Makes 18 | Prep time 8–10 minutes | Cooking time 20 minutes

Ingredients
1 cup sugar
2 cups flour
½ teaspoon salt
1 tablespoon baking powder
2 eggs, slightly beaten
½ cup oil
1 cup light cream
1 teaspoon lemon extract
1 ½ cups red raspberries
Cooking spray or vegetable oil for greasing (optional)

Directions

1. Preheat an oven to 375°F (190°C).
2. Line a muffin pan with muffin liners or grease each hole with cooking spray or vegetable oil.
3. In a bowl, thoroughly mix the dry ingredients.
4. Add in the wet ingredients and mix well.
5. Mix in the raspberries last and combine well to form a moist mixture.
6. Transfer the batter to the muffin pan, filling the liners just ¾ full to allow room for the muffins to rise.
7. Bake for 20 minutes or until a toothpick inserted in the center comes out clean.
8. Remove from the oven and let the muffins rest in the pan for 5 minutes. Then, transfer to a wire rack to cool down.

Nutrition (per serving)
Calories. 174, carbs 22 g, fat 8.8 g,
Protein 2.2 g, sodium 76 mg

Raspberry Yogurt Muffins

Makes 12 | Prep time 10 minutes | Cooking time 17 minutes

Ingredients
1 ½ cups all-purpose flour
¼ cup cornstarch
1 ½ cup granulated sugar
2 ½ teaspoons baking powder
½ teaspoon salt
¾ cup vegetable oil
1 cup Greek yogurt
2 large eggs, room temperature
2 teaspoons vanilla extract
1 cup fresh or frozen raspberries
Cooking spray or vegetable oil for greasing (optional)

Directions

1. Preheat the oven at 350°F (177°C).
2. Line a muffin pan with muffin liners or grease each hole with cooking spray or vegetable oil.
3. In a mixing bowl, mix the flour, baking powder, cornstarch, and salt.
4. In another large bowl, mix the vegetable oil and the granulated sugar.
5. Stir in the eggs, Greek yogurt and mix until combined. Stir in vanilla extract.
6. Add the dry ingredients to the wet ingredients and mix until combined. Be careful not to overmix the batter.
7. Transfer the batter to the muffin pan, filling the liners just ¾ full to allow room for the muffins to rise.
8. Top each muffin with fresh or frozen raspberries.

9. Bake in the oven for about 15-17 minutes or until a toothpick inserted in the center comes out clean.
10. Remove from the oven and let the muffins rest in the pan for 5 minutes. Then, transfer to a wire rack to cool down.
11. Serve and enjoy.

Nutrition (per serving)
Calories 330, fat 15 g, carbs 46.1 g,
Protein 4.5 g, sodium 116 mg

Blackberry Muffins

Makes 10 | Prep time 10 minutes | Cooking time 25 minutes

Ingredients

2½ cups blanched all-purpose flour, finely ground and sifted
⅓ cup granulated sweetener
¼ teaspoon salt
1½ teaspoons baking powder
⅓ cup unsweetened almond or cashew milk
⅓ cup coconut oil or melted butter
½ teaspoon vanilla extract
3 large eggs
¾ cup blackberries or raspberries, fresh or frozen and thawed
Cooking spray or vegetable oil for greasing (optional)

Directions

1. Preheat the oven to 350°F (177°C). Line a muffin pan with muffin liners or grease each hole with cooking spray or vegetable oil.
2. Add the granulated sweetener, all-purpose flour, baking powder, and salt to a mixing bowl. Mix well.
3. Mix in the berries.
4. In another large bowl beat the eggs. Add the vanilla extract, coconut oil or butter, and almond milk. Mix well.
5. Combine the mixtures and mix well until no visible lumps remain.
6. Transfer the batter to the muffin pan, filling the liners just ¾ full to allow room for the muffins to rise.
7. Bake for 25 minutes or until a toothpick inserted in the center comes out clean.
8. Remove from the oven and let the muffins rest in the pan for 5 minutes. Then, transfer to a wire rack to cool down.

9. Gently remove muffins from cups; serve fresh.

Nutrition (per serving)
Calories 277, fat 25 g, carbs 8 g,
Protein 8 g, sodium 101 mg

Strawberry Rhubarb Muffins

Makes 12 | Prep time 15 minutes |Cooking time 25 minutes

Ingredients

3 cups flour
½ cup brown sugar
1 tablespoon baking powder
½ teaspoon baking soda
1 teaspoon salt
½ cup butter, softened
2 eggs
1 cup buttermilk
½ cup skim milk
1 ½ cups rhubarb, diced
1 ½ cups fresh strawberries, diced
½ cup zucchini, shredded
1 teaspoon lemon zest
Cooking spray or vegetable oil for greasing (optional)

Directions

1. Preheat the oven to 375°F (190°C).
2. Line a muffin pan with muffin liners or grease each hole with cooking spray or vegetable oil.
3. In one bowl, combine the flour, sugar, baking powder, baking soda, and salt.
4. In a separate bowl, combine the butter and the eggs. Use an electric mixer on medium-low speed to completely blend the two ingredients.
5. In alternating additions, add in the dry ingredients and then the buttermilk and skim milk into the butter and egg mixture.
6. Next, fold in the rhubarb, strawberries, zucchini, and lemon zest.

7. Transfer the batter to the muffin pan, filling the liners just ¾ full to allow room for the muffins to rise.
8. Bake for 25 minutes or until a toothpick inserted in the center comes out clean.
9. *Remove from the oven and let the muffins rest in the pan for 5 minutes. Then, transfer to a wire rack to cool down.*

Nutrition (per serving)
Calories 181, fat 7 g, carbs 26 g,
Protein 4 g, sodium 7 g

Strawberry Muffins

Makes 12 | Prep time 10 minutes | Cooking time 15 minutes

Ingredients

1 ½ cups all-purpose flour
2 tablespoons cornstarch
1 cup granulated sugar
2 ½ teaspoons baking powder
½ teaspoon salt
¾ cup vegetable oil
1 cup whole milk
2 large eggs, room temperature
2 teaspoons vanilla extract
7 ounces fresh or frozen strawberries, diced into slices
Cooking spray or vegetable oil for greasing (optional)

Directions

1. Preheat the oven at 350°F (177°C).
2. Line a muffin pan with muffin liners or grease each hole with cooking spray or vegetable oil.
3. In a mixing bowl, mix the flour, baking powder, cornstarch, and salt.
4. In another mix the vegetable oil with the sugar.
5. Stir in the eggs, whole milk and mix until combined.
6. Stir in vanilla extract.
7. Add the dry ingredients to the wet ingredients and mix until combined. Be careful not to overmix the batter.
8. Transfer the batter to the muffin pan, filling the liners just ¾ full to allow room for the muffins to rise.
9. Arrange sliced strawberries on top of each muffin.
10. Bake in the oven for about 20 minutes or until a toothpick comes out clean.

11. Remove from the oven and let the muffins rest in the pan for 5 minutes. Then, transfer to a wire rack to cool down.
12. Serve and enjoy with powdered sugar if desired.

Nutrition (per serving)

Calories 278, fat 15.3 g, carbs 32.8 g,
Protein 3.3 g, sodium 118 mg

Whole Grain and Dried Fruit Muffins

Makes 12 | Prep time 15 minutes I Cooking time 15 minutes

Ingredients

1 ½ cups whole wheat flour
2 teaspoons baking powder
½ teaspoon cinnamon
¼ teaspoon nutmeg
¼ teaspoon ground ginger
2 eggs
1 tablespoon honey, or preferred sugar substitute
1 teaspoon pure vanilla extract
¼ cup coconut oil, liquefied
½ cup unsweetened apple juice
¼ cup orange juice
¼ cup dates, chopped
¼ cup dried cranberries
¼ cup dried apricots, chopped
½ cup unsalted pistachios, chopped
Cooking spray or vegetable oil for greasing (optional)

Directions

1. Preheat the oven to 400°F (204°C).
2. Line a muffin pan with muffin liners or grease each hole with cooking spray or vegetable oil.
3. In a bowl, combine the whole wheat flour, baking powder, cinnamon, nutmeg, and ginger.
4. In another large bowl, lightly beat the eggs and add the honey, vanilla extract, coconut oil, apple juice, and orange juice.
5. Add the wet and dry ingredients together, mixing only until blended. The mixture will likely be somewhat lumpy.

Make sure to not over-mix.

6. Fold in the dates, cranberries, apricots, and pistachios.
7. Transfer the batter to the muffin pan, filling the liners just ¾ full to allow room for the muffins to rise.
8. Place in the oven and bake for 12-15 minutes, or until a pick inserted in the center comes out clean.
9. Remove from the oven and let the muffins rest in the pan for 5 minutes. Then, transfer to a wire rack to cool down.

Nutrition (per serving)
Calories 173, fat 7.9 g, carbs 23.3 g,
Protein 4.3 g, sodium 94 mg,

FUN FLAVORS

Nutella™ Muffins

Makes 12 | Prep time 10 minutes | Cooking time 15 minutes

Ingredients
¾ cups all-purpose flour
½ cup cocoa powder
¾ cup granulated sugar
½ cup chocolate hazelnut spread like Nutella™
¾ teaspoon baking powder
½ teaspoon baking soda
⅓ cup vegetable oil
2 large eggs, room temperature
2 teaspoons vanilla extract
½ cup whole milk
Cooking spray or vegetable oil for greasing (optional)

Directions

1. Preheat the oven at 350°F (177°C).
2. Line a muffin pan with muffin liners or grease each hole with cooking spray or vegetable oil.
3. In a mixing bowl, mix the flour, baking powder, and baking soda.
4. In another large bowl, with the help of a hand mixer, beat in the butter, Nutella, and granulated sugar until creamy and fluffy. It will take around 7 minutes.
5. Stir in the eggs, one at a time, mixing well between each addition.
6. Then alternatively add the whole milk with the dry ingredients and mix until combined. Be careful not to overmix the batter.

7. Stir in the vanilla extract.
8. Transfer the batter to the muffin pan, filling the liners just ¾ full to allow room for the muffins to rise.
9. Bake in the oven for about 12-15 minutes or until a toothpick inserted in the center comes out clean.
10. Remove from the oven and let the muffins rest in the pan for 5 minutes. Then, transfer to a wire rack to cool down.
11. To make them even more special spread just a teaspoon of Nutella on top of each muffin just right before serving.

Nutrition (per serving)
Calories 191, fat 9.6 g, carbs 25 g,

Protein 3.2 g, sodium 71 mg

Funfetti Muffins

Makes 12 | Prep time 10 minutes | Cooking time 15 minutes

Ingredients

1 ⅔ cups all-purpose flour
1 cup granulated sugar
1 teaspoon baking powder
½ cup butter, soften
1 large egg, room temperature
2 teaspoons vanilla extract
1 cup buttermilk
½ cup rainbow sprinkles
Cooking spray or vegetable oil for greasing (optional)

Directions

1. Preheat the oven at 350°F (177°C).
2. Line a muffin pan with muffin liners or grease each hole with cooking spray or vegetable oil.
3. In a mixing bowl, mix the flour, and baking powder.
4. In another large bowl, with the help of a hand mixer, beat in the butter and granulated sugar until creamy and pale yellow. It will take around 7 minutes.
5. Stir in the egg, and mix until combined.
6. Then add the buttermilk and vanilla extract. Be careful not to overmix the batter.
7. Stir in the sprinkles.
8. Transfer the batter to the muffin pan, filling the liners just ¾ full to allow room for the muffins to rise.
9. Bake in the oven for about 12-15 minutes or until a toothpick inserted in the center comes out clean.
10. Remove from the oven and let the muffins rest in the pan for 5 minutes. Then, transfer to a wire rack to cool down.

Nutrition (per serving)
Calories 213, fat 8.4 g, carbs 32.8 g,
Protein 3.3 g, sodium 89 mg

Chocolate and Peanut Butter Muffins

Makes 14 I Prep time 10 minutes I Cooking time 20 minutes

Ingredients

¾ cups all-purpose flour
½ cup cocoa powder
1 cup granulated sugar
1 ¼ teaspoons baking powder
⅓ cup vegetable oil
2 large eggs, room temperature
2 teaspoons vanilla extract
½ cup whole milk
¼ cup peanut butter, softened
Cooking spray or vegetable oil for greasing (optional)

Directions

1. Preheat the oven at 350°F (177°C).
2. Line a muffin pan with muffin liners or grease each hole with cooking spray or vegetable oil.
3. In a mixing bowl, mix the flour, and baking powder.
4. In another large bowl, mix the vegetable oil with the granulated sugar until combined.
5. Stir in the eggs, one at a time, mixing well between each addition.
6. Then alternatively add the whole milk, smooth peanut butter, and the dry ingredients and mix until combined. Be careful not to overmix the batter.
7. Stir in the vanilla extract.
8. Transfer the batter to the muffin pan, filling the liners just ¾ full to allow room for the muffins to rise.
9. Bake in the oven for about 12-15 minutes or until a toothpick inserted in the center comes out clean.

10. Remove from the oven and let the muffins rest in the pan for 5 minutes. Then, transfer to a wire rack to cool down.
11. Serve and enjoy.

Nutrition (per serving)
Calories 205, fat 10.5 g, carbs 26.5 g,
Protein 4.2 g, sodium 42 mg

Brownie Muffins

Makes 12 I Prep time 10 minutes I Cooking time 15 minutes

Ingredients

¾ cups all-purpose flour
½ cup cocoa powder
¾ cup granulated sugar
½ cup light brown sugar
¾ teaspoon baking powder
½ teaspoon baking soda
⅓ cup vegetable oil
2 large eggs, room temperature
2 teaspoons vanilla extract
½ cup whole milk
Cooking spray or vegetable oil for greasing (optional)

Directions

1. Preheat the oven at 350°F (177°C).
2. Line a muffin pan with muffin liners or grease each hole with cooking spray or vegetable oil.
3. In a mixing bowl, mix the flour, cocoa powder, baking powder, and baking soda.
4. In another large bowl, with the help of a hand mixer, beat in the butter, light brown sugar, and granulated sugar until creamy and fluffy. It will take around 7 minutes.
5. Stir in the eggs, one at a time, mixing well between each addition.
6. Then alternatively add the whole milk with the dry ingredients and mix until combined. Be careful not to overmix the batter.
7. Stir in the vanilla extract.

8. Transfer the batter to the muffin pan, filling the liners just ¾ full to allow room for the muffins to rise.
9. Bake in the oven for about 12-15 minutes. You still want that center to be fudgy and not baked the whole way through.
10. Serve and enjoy.

Nutrition (per serving)
Calories 180, fat 7.8 g, carbs 27.1 g,
Protein 2.9 g, sodium 71 mg

Mocha Muffins

Makes 16 I Prep time 10 minutes I Cooking time 20 minutes

Ingredients
½ cup espresso
2 teaspoons instant espresso powder
½ cup whole milk
1 teaspoon vanilla extract
1 ⅓ cup all-purpose flour
⅓ cup cocoa powder
1 ½ teaspoon baking powder
½ cup butter, room temperature
½ cup granulated sugar
1 large egg, room temperature
Cooking spray or vegetable oil for greasing (optional)

Directions

1. Preheat the oven at 350°F (177°C).
2. Line a muffin pan with muffin liners or grease each hole with cooking spray or vegetable oil.
3. In a mixing bowl, mix the coffee, instant espresso powder, whole milk, and vanilla extract.
4. In another large bowl, beat up the butter with the granulated sugar and stir in the egg.
5. Then, pour in the espresso mixture into the butter mixture and mix until clumpy and lumpy.
6. In a third bowl, combine the flour, cocoa powder, baking powder, and stir them into the wet ingredients.
7. Transfer the batter to the muffin pan, filling the liners just ¾ full to allow room for the muffins to rise.
8. Bake in the oven for about 12-15 minutes or until a toothpick inserted in the center comes out clean.

9. Remove from the oven and let the muffins rest in the pan for 5 minutes. Then, transfer to a wire rack to cool down.
10. Serve and enjoy.

Nutrition (per serving)
Calories 169, fat 8.9 g, carbs 21.1 g,
Protein 2.8 g, sodium 67 mg

Peanut Butter Muffins

Makes 12 | Prep time 10 minutes | Cooking time 15 minutes

Ingredients

1 ½ cups all-purpose flour
1 ¼ cup granulated sugar
1 teaspoon baking powder
⅓ cup vegetable oil
1 large egg, room temperature
3 tablespoons peanut butter
2 teaspoons vanilla extract
½ cup buttermilk
Cooking spray or vegetable oil for greasing (optional)

Directions

1. Preheat the oven at 350°F (177°C).
2. Line a muffin pan with muffin liners or grease each hole with cooking spray or vegetable oil.
3. In a mixing bowl, mix the flour and baking powder.
4. In another large bowl, with the help of a spatula mix the oil and granulated sugar until combined.
5. Stir in the egg and peanut butter.
6. Then alternatively add the buttermilk with the dry ingredients and mix until combined. Be careful not to overmix the batter.
7. Stir in the vanilla extract.
8. Transfer the batter to the muffin pan, filling the liners just ¾ full to allow room for the muffins to rise.
9. Bake in the oven for about 12-15 minutes or until a toothpick inserted in the center comes out clean.
10. Remove from the oven and let the muffins rest in the pan for 5 minutes. Then, transfer to a wire rack to cool down.

11. Serve and enjoy.

Nutrition (per serving)
Calories 225, fat 8.7 g, carbs 34.4 g,
Protein 3.5 g, sodium 36 mg

Cocoa and White Chocolate Muffins

Makes 12 I Prep time 10 minutes I Cooking time 15 minutes

Ingredients

¾ cups all-purpose flour
½ cup cocoa powder
1 ¼ cup light brown sugar
1 teaspoon baking powder
⅓ cup vegetable oil
2 large eggs, room temperature
½ cup whole milk
2 teaspoons vanilla extract
¾ cup white chocolate chips
Cooking spray or vegetable oil for greasing (optional)

Directions

1. Preheat the oven at 350°F (177°C).
2. Line a muffin pan with muffin liners or grease each hole with cooking spray or vegetable oil.
3. In a mixing bowl, mix the flour, cocoa powder, and baking powder
4. In another large bowl, with the help of a spatula mix the oil and light brown sugar until combined.
5. Stir in the eggs and mix until combined.
6. Then alternatively add the whole milk with the dry ingredients and mix until combined. Be careful not to overmix the batter.
7. Stir in the vanilla extract and the white chocolate chips.
8. Transfer the batter to the muffin pan, filling the liners just ¾ full to allow room for the muffins to rise.
9. Bake in the oven for about 12-15 minutes or until a toothpick inserted in the center comes out clean.

10. Remove from the oven and let the muffins rest in the pan for 5 minutes. Then, transfer to a wire rack to cool down.
11. Serve and enjoy.

Nutrition (per serving)
Calories 168, fat 7.8 g, carbs 23.5 g,
Protein 2.9 g, sodium 21 mg

Peanut Butter Banana Muffins

Makes 12 | Prep time 15 minutes | Cooking time 15 minutes

Ingredients

1 ½ cups all-purpose flour
1 ¼ cup granulated sugar
1 ½ teaspoon baking powder
⅓ cup vegetable oil
1 large egg, room temperature
2 tablespoons peanut butter
2 teaspoons vanilla extract
½ cup mashed bananas
½ cup whole milk
Cooking spray or vegetable oil for greasing (optional)

Directions

1. Preheat the oven at 350°F (177°C).
2. Line a muffin pan with muffin liners or grease each hole with cooking spray or vegetable oil.
3. In a mixing bowl, mix the flour and baking powder.
4. In another large bowl, with the help of a spatula mix the oil and granulated sugar until combined.
5. Stir in the egg and peanut butter.
6. Then alternatively add the whole milk with the dry ingredients and mix until combined. Be careful not to overmix the batter.
7. Stir in the vanilla extract.
8. Transfer the batter to the muffin pan, filling the liners just ¾ full to allow room for the muffins to rise.
9. Bake in the oven for about 12-15 minutes or until a toothpick inserted in the center comes out clean.

10. Remove from the oven and let the muffins rest in the pan for 5 minutes. Then, transfer to a wire rack to cool down.
11. Serve and enjoy.

Nutrition (per serving)
Calories 225, fat 8.3 g, carbs 35.6 g,
Protein 3.2 g, sodium 23 mg

Maple Bacon Muffins

Makes 12 | Prep time 10 minutes | Cooking time 15 minutes

Ingredients
1 ½ cup all-purpose flour
1 ½ teaspoon baking powder
Pinch of salt
½ cup butter, softened
1 cup light brown sugar
2 large eggs, room temperature
1 teaspoon vanilla extract
⅓ cup maple syrup
⅓ cup whole milk
3 ounces bacon, diced and fried
Cooking spray or vegetable oil for greasing (optional)

Directions

1. Preheat the oven at 350°F (177°C).
2. Line a muffin pan with muffin liners or grease each hole with cooking spray or vegetable oil.
3. In a mixing bowl, mix the flour, baking soda, salt, and baking powder
4. In another large bowl, with the help of a spatula mix in the butter with the light brown sugar.
5. Stir in the eggs and mix until combined. Stir in the whole milk and maple syrup.
6. Then add the dry ingredients and mix until combined. Be careful not to overmix the batter.
7. Stir in the vanilla extract and fried bacon pieces.
8. Transfer the batter to the muffin pan, filling the liners just ¾ full to allow room for the muffins to rise.

9. Bake in the oven for about 12-15 minutes or until a toothpick inserted in the center comes out clean.
10. Remove from the oven and let the muffins rest in the pan for 5 minutes. Then, transfer to a wire rack to cool down.
11. Serve and enjoy.

Nutrition (per serving)
Calories 249, fat 11.9 g, carbs 30.5 g,

Protein 5.6 g, sodium 249 mg

Amish Friendship Muffins

Makes 12 | Prep time 10 minutes | Cooking time 20 minutes

Ingredients
1 cup sugar
½ cup butter, softened
1 egg
1 cup buttermilk
2 cups flour
1 teaspoon vanilla
1 teaspoon baking soda
Cooking spray or vegetable oil for greasing (optional)

Cinnamon mixture
1 teaspoon cinnamon
⅓ cup sugar

Directions

1. Preheat an oven to 350ºF (177°C).
2. Line a muffin pan with muffin liners or grease each hole with cooking spray or vegetable oil.
3. In a medium bowl, thoroughly mix the sugar, butter, vanilla, and egg.
4. Add in the baking soda, flour, and milk; combine well.
5. In another large bowl, thoroughly mix the cinnamon and sugar to make the cinnamon mixture.
6. Transfer the batter to the muffin pan, filling the liners just ¾ full to allow room for the muffins to rise.
7. Bake for 20–25 minutes or until a toothpick inserted in the center comes out clean.
8. Remove from the oven and let the muffins rest in the pan for 5 minutes. Then, transfer to a wire rack to cool down.
9. Take out, cool down for a few minutes, and serve warm!

Nutrition (per serving)
Calories 221, carbs 33g, fat 8.4g,
Protein 3.4g, sodium 186mg

Sour Cream Chocolate Chip Muffins

Makes 12 I Prep time 10 minutes I Cooking time 20 minutes

Ingredients

¾ cups all-purpose flour
½ cup cocoa powder
¾ cup granulated sugar
½ cup light brown sugar
¾ teaspoon baking powder
⅓ cup vegetable oil
2 large eggs, room temperature
2 teaspoons vanilla extract
½ cup sour cream
1 cup chocolate chips
Cooking spray or vegetable oil for greasing (optional)

Directions

1. Preheat the oven at 350°F (177°C).
2. Line a muffin pan with muffin liners or grease each hole with cooking spray or vegetable oil.
3. In a mixing bowl, mix the flour, cocoa powder, baking powder, and baking soda.
4. In another large bowl, with the help of a hand mixer, beat in the butter, light brown sugar, and granulated sugar until creamy and fluffy. It will take around 7 minutes.
5. Stir in the eggs, one at a time, mixing well between each addition.
6. Then alternatively add the sour cream with the dry ingredients and mix until combined. Be careful not to overmix the batter.
7. Stir in the vanilla extract.
8. Fold in the chocolate chips.

9. Transfer the batter to the muffin pan, filling the liners just ¾ full to allow room for the muffins to rise.
10. Bake in the oven for about 20 minutes or until a toothpick inserted in the center comes out clean.
11. Remove from the oven and let the muffins rest in the pan for 5 minutes. Then, transfer to a wire rack to cool down.
12. Serve to enjoy.

Nutrition (per serving)

Calories 269, fat 13.6 g, carbs 35.4 g,

Protein 3.9 g, sodium 31 mg

Cinnamon Muffins

Makes 12 | Prep time 15 minutes | Cooking time 15 minutes

Ingredients

1 ½ cup all-purpose flour
1 teaspoon baking powder
½ teaspoon baking soda
1 tablespoon ground cinnamon
Pinch of salt
½ cup vegetable oil
½ cup light brown sugar
¼ cup granulated sugar
2 large eggs, room temperature
1 teaspoon vanilla extract
¾ cup whole milk
Cooking spray or vegetable oil for greasing (optional)

Directions

1. Preheat the oven at 350°F (177°C).
2. Line a muffin pan with muffin liners or grease each hole with cooking spray or vegetable oil.
3. In a mixing bowl, mix the flour, baking soda, ground cinnamon, salt, and baking powder
4. In another large bowl, with the help of a wire whisk the vegetable oil with the light brown sugar and granulated sugar.
5. Stir in the eggs and mix until combined. It will be lumpy and clumpy but that's totally fine. Stir in the whole milk.
6. Then add the dry ingredients and mix until combined. Be careful not to overmix the batter.
7. Stir in the vanilla extract.

8. Transfer the batter to the muffin pan, filling the liners just ¾ full to allow room for the muffins to rise.
9. Bake in the oven for about 12-15 minutes or until a toothpick inserted in the center comes out clean.
10. Remove from the oven and let the muffins rest in the pan for 5 minutes. Then, transfer to a wire rack to cool down.
11. Serve and enjoy.

Nutrition (per serving)
Calories 200, fat 10.6 g, carbs 23.5 g,
Protein 3.2 g, sodium 84 mg

Oatmeal Raisin Cinnamon Muffins

Makes 12 | Prep time 10–15 minutes | Cooking time 20 minutes

Ingredients
1 large egg, beaten
¼ cup sugar
½ teaspoon salt
½ cup chopped raisins
1 teaspoon ground cinnamon
1 cup quick-cooking rolled oats
1 teaspoon vanilla extract
1 cup flour, all-purpose
3/4 cup milk
1 tablespoon baking powder
3 tablespoons vegetable oil
Cooking spray or vegetable oil for greasing (optional)

Topping
1 teaspoon margarine, melted
2 teaspoons flour, all-purpose
2 tablespoons sugar
1 teaspoon ground cinnamon

Directions

1. Preheat an oven to 350ºF (180°C).
2. Line a muffin pan with muffin liners or grease each hole with cooking spray or vegetable oil.
3. In a large bowl, thoroughly mix the flour, cinnamon, sugar, baking powder, and salt. Mix in the raisins and rolled oats.
4. In another large bowl, thoroughly mix the vanilla, milk, egg, and oil.

5. Add the dry ingredients to the wet ingredients and mix until combined.
6. Take a separate medium bowl and thoroughly mix the topping ingredients.
7. Transfer the batter to the muffin pan, filling the liners just ¾ full to allow room for the muffins to rise.
8. Bake in the oven for about 12-15 minutes or until a toothpick inserted in the center comes out clean.
9. Remove from the oven and let the muffins rest in the pan for 5 minutes. Then, transfer to a wire rack to cool down.
10. Take out, cool down for a few minutes, and serve warm!

Nutrition (per serving)
Calories 144, carbs 23g, fat 4.7g,
Protein 3g, sodium 112mg

Brown Sugar Oat Muffins

Makes 12 I Prep time 10 minutes I Cooking time 15 minutes

Ingredients
2 cups old fashioned oats
1 cup whole milk
½ cup maple syrup
⅓ cup melted butter
⅔ cup light brown sugar
2 large eggs, room temperature
1 ¼ cup all-purpose flour
1 teaspoon baking powder
1 teaspoon ground cinnamon
Pinch of salt
Cooking spray or vegetable oil for greasing (optional)

Directions

1. Preheat the oven at 350°F (177°C).
2. Line a muffin pan with muffin liners or grease each hole with cooking spray or vegetable oil.
3. In a mixing bowl, mix the flour, oats, cinnamon, and baking powder.
4. In another large bowl, with the help of a spatula mix in the melted butter, eggs, light brown sugar, maple syrup, and salt.
5. Add the dry ingredients to the wet ingredients and mix until combined. Be careful not to overmix the batter. Stir in the vanilla extract.
6. Transfer the batter to the muffin pan, filling the liners just ¾ full to allow room for the muffins to rise.
7. Bake in the oven for about 12-15 minutes or until a toothpick inserted in the center comes out clean.

8. Remove from the oven and let the muffins rest in the pan for 5 minutes. Then, transfer to a wire rack to cool down.
9. Serve and enjoy.

Nutrition (per serving)
Calories 287, fat 8.5 g, carbs 45.9 g,
Protein 6.4 g, sodium 72 mg

VEGGIE-BASED MUFFINS

Carrot Walnut Muffins

Makes 14 I Prep time 10 minutes I Cooking time 20 minutes

Ingredients
1 ¼ cup all-purpose flour
1 teaspoon baking soda
1 teaspoon cinnamon
½ cup vegetable oil
½ cup granulated sugar
½ cup light brown sugar
1 teaspoon vanilla extract
2 large eggs, room temperature
1 ½ cups carrots, grated
⅓ cup walnuts, chopped
¼ cup raisins
Cooking spray or vegetable oil for greasing (optional)

Directions

1. Preheat the oven at 350°F (177°C).
2. Line a muffin pan with muffin liners or grease each hole with cooking spray or vegetable oil.
3. In a mixing bowl, mix the flour, cinnamon, and baking soda.
4. In another large bowl, with the help of a hand mixer mix the oil, granulated sugar, light brown sugar, eggs, and carrots.
5. Then add the dry ingredients and mix until combined. Be careful not to overmix the batter. Stir in the chopped walnuts and raisins.

6. Transfer the batter to the muffin pan, filling the liners just ¾ full to allow room for the muffins to rise.
7. Bake in the oven for about 12-15 minutes or until a toothpick inserted in the center comes out clean.
8. Remove from the oven and let the muffins rest in the pan for 5 minutes. Then, transfer to a wire rack to cool down.
9. Serve and enjoy.

Nutrition (per serving)

Calories 214, fat 11.2 g, carbs 26.4 g,

Protein 3.2 g, sodium 117 mg

Carrot Cake Muffins

Makes 12 | Prep time 8 minutes | Cooking time 20 minutes

Ingredients

1 cup all-purpose flour
½ teaspoon baking soda
½ teaspoon baking powder
Pinch of salt
½ teaspoon ground cinnamon
¼ teaspoon ground nutmeg
1 cup sugar
2 large eggs
½ cup melted butter
1 teaspoon vanilla extract
3 medium carrots, peeled and grated
½ cup chopped almonds
½ cup coconut flakes
Cooking spray or vegetable oil for greasing (optional)

Directions

1. Preheat the oven at 350°F (177°C)
2. Line a muffin pan with muffin liners or grease each hole with cooking spray or vegetable oil.
3. Add the flour, baking soda, baking powder, salt, cinnamon, and nutmeg to a bowl.
4. Stir until mixed and set aside.
5. In another large bowl, mix the sugar, eggs, melted butter, and vanilla until combined.
6. Stir in the grated carrots, almonds, and coconut.
7. Stir in the dry ingredients and mix until just combined.
8. Transfer the batter to the muffin pan, filling the liners just ¾ full to allow room for the muffins to rise.

9. Bake for 25 minutes or until a toothpick inserted in the center comes out clean.
10. Remove from the oven and let the muffins rest in the pan for 5 minutes. Then, transfer to a wire rack to cool down.
11. Gently remove muffins from cups; serve fresh.

Nutrition (per serving)
Calories 223, fat 11.7 g, carbs 27.8 g,
Protein 3.3 g, sodium 141 mg

Zucchini Chocolate Muffins

Makes 12 | Prep time 10 minutes | Cooking time 25 minutes

Ingredients
¼ teaspoon salt
½ teaspoon baking soda
2 cups all-purpose flour
¼ cup unsweetened cocoa
¼ cup vegetable oil
¼ cup white sugar
3 large eggs
½ cup semi-sweet chocolate chips
¾ cup shredded zucchini
Cooking spray or vegetable oil for greasing (optional)

Directions

1. Preheat the oven to 350°F (177°C). Line a muffin pan with muffin liners or grease each hole with cooking spray or vegetable oil.
2. Add the flour, salt, cocoa, and baking soda to a mixing bowl. Mix well.
3. In another large bowl, beat the eggs. Add the sugar and oil. Mix well.
4. Mix in the zucchini and chocolate chips.
5. Add the dry ingredients to the wet ingredients and mix until combined.
6. Transfer the batter to the muffin pan, filling the liners just ¾ full to allow room for the muffins to rise.
7. Bake in the oven for about 12-15 minutes or until a toothpick inserted in the center comes out clean.
8. Let cool inside the oven for 5 minutes.

9. Remove from oven and let muffins cool on a wire rack for about 10 minutes before serving.

Nutrition (per serving)
Calories 247, fat 16 g, carbs 14 g,
Protein 6 g, sodium 117 mg

Pumpkin Muffins

Makes 12 | Prep time 10 minutes | Cooking time 20 minutes

Ingredients

1 ¼ cup all-purpose flour
1 ½ teaspoon baking powder
Pinch of salt
1 cup pumpkin puree
¾ cup vegetable oil
1 cup granulated sugar
2 large eggs, room temperature
1 teaspoon vanilla extract
Cooking spray or vegetable oil for greasing (optional)

Directions

1. Preheat the oven at 350°F (177°C).
2. Line a muffin pan with muffin liners or grease each hole with cooking spray or vegetable oil.
3. Then, in a mixing bowl, mix the flour, baking powder, and salt.
4. In another large bowl, with the wire whisk mix the pumpkin puree, vegetable oil, and granulated sugar until combined.
5. Stir in the eggs and mix vigorously. Mix in the vanilla extract.
6. Add the dry ingredients and fold them together with the wet ingredients.
7. Transfer the batter to the muffin pan, filling the liners just ¾ full to allow room for the muffins to rise.
8. Bake in the oven for about 12-15 minutes or until a toothpick inserted in the center comes out clean.

9. Remove from the oven and let the muffins rest in the pan for 5 minutes. Then, transfer to a wire rack to cool down.
10. Serve and enjoy.

Nutrition (per serving)
Calories 251, fat 14.7 g, carbs 28.7 g,
Protein 2.6 g, sodium 25 mg

Pumpkin Chocolate Chip Muffins

Makes 12 | Prep time 10 minutes | Cooking time 15 minutes

Ingredients

1 ¼ cup all-purpose flour
1 teaspoon baking powder
½ teaspoon baking soda
Pinch of salt
¾ cup pumpkin puree
¾ cup vegetable oil
1 cup granulated sugar
2 large eggs, room temperature
1 teaspoon vanilla extract
1 cup chocolate chips
Cooking spray or vegetable oil for greasing (optional)

Directions

1. Preheat the oven at 350°F (177°C).
2. Line a muffin pan with muffin liners or grease each hole with cooking spray or vegetable oil.
3. Then, in a mixing bowl mix the flour, baking powder, baking soda, and salt together.
4. In another large bowl, with the wire whisk mix the pumpkin puree, vegetable oil, and granulated sugar until combined.
5. Stir in the eggs and mix vigorously. Mix in the vanilla extract and fold in the chocolate chips.
6. Add the dry ingredients and fold them together with the wet ingredients.
7. Transfer the batter to the muffin pan, filling the liners just ¾ full to allow room for the muffins to rise.

8. Bake in the oven for about 12-15 minutes or until a toothpick inserted in the center comes out clean.
9. Remove from the oven and let the muffins rest in the pan for 5 minutes. Then, transfer to a wire rack to cool down.
10. Serve and enjoy.

Nutrition (per serving)

Calories 324, fat 18.8 g, carbs 36.5 g,

Protein 3.6 g, sodium 88 mg

Pumpkin Crumble Muffins

Makes 12 I Prep time 10 minutes I Cooking time 20 minutes

Ingredients
<u>For the muffins</u>
1 ¼ cup all-purpose flour
1 ½ teaspoon baking powder
1 teaspoon ground cinnamon
Pinch of salt
1 cup pumpkin puree
½ cup vegetable oil
¾ cup granulated sugar
2 large eggs, room temperature
1 teaspoon vanilla extract
Cooking spray or vegetable oil for greasing (optional)

<u>For the crumble topping</u>
2 tablespoons butter, cold
1 tablespoon light brown sugar
3 tablespoons all-purpose flour
pinch of cinnamon

Directions

1. Preheat the oven at 350°F (177°C).
2. Line a muffin pan with muffin liners or grease each hole with cooking spray or vegetable oil.
3. Then, in a mixing bowl mix the flour, baking powder, ground cinnamon, and salt together.
4. In another with the wire whisk mix the pumpkin puree, vegetable oil, and granulated sugar until combined.
5. Stir in the eggs and mix vigorously.
6. Mix in the vanilla extract.

7. Add the dry ingredients and fold them together with the wet ingredients.
8. Transfer the batter to the muffin pan, filling the liners just ¾ full to allow room for the muffins to rise.
9. In a small bowl mix the flour, light brown sugar, flour, ground cinnamon, and butter.
10. Rub with your finger to make the crumble topping and top each muffin with the crumble.
11. Bake in the oven for about 12-15 minutes or until a toothpick inserted in the center comes out clean.
12. Remove from the oven and let the muffins rest in the pan for 5 minutes. Then, transfer to a wire rack to cool down.
13. Serve and enjoy.

Nutrition (per serving)
Calories 215, fat 12 g, carbs 25.4 g,
Protein 2.6 g, sodium 39 mg

Pumpkin Cream Muffins

Makes 18 | Prep time 8–10 minutes | Cooking time 15 minutes

Ingredients

Dough
¼ teaspoon baking soda
5/8 cup sugar
1 egg
6 tablespoons butter
1 teaspoon baking powder
1 teaspoon vanilla
3/8 cup milk
2 cups flour
Cooking spray or vegetable oil for greasing (optional)

Filling
½ cup fresh diced pumpkin
4 ounces cream cheese
¼ cup sugar
¼ teaspoon nutmeg
½ teaspoon cinnamon

Frosting
½ teaspoon vanilla
4 ounces cream cheese
2 cups powdered sugar

Directions

1. Preheat an oven to 350°F (177°C).
2. Line a muffin pan with muffin liners or grease each hole with cooking spray or vegetable oil.
3. In a blender, puree the pumpkin.

4. In a mixing bowl, gently whisk the sugar, pumpkin puree, cinnamon, nutmeg, and cream cheese to make the filling.
5. In another large bowl, thoroughly mix the dough ingredients.
6. Divide the prepared dough and form it into mini pies.
7. Add the mini pies to the muffin pan.
8. Fill evenly with the pumpkin mixture.
9. Bake for 25 minutes or until a toothpick inserted in the center comes out clean.
10. Remove from the oven and let the muffins rest in the pan for 5 minutes. Then, transfer to a wire rack to cool down.
11. In a medium bowl, thoroughly mix the frosting ingredients.
12. Add the mixture to a zip-lock bag and cut one corner.
13. Pour on top of muffins. Serve warm!

Nutrition (per serving)
Calories 204mg, carbs 26g, fat 9.8g,
Protein 3.7g, sodium 105mg

Sweet Potato Muffins

Makes 12 | Prep time 10 minutes | Cooking time 15 minutes

Ingredients
1 cup all-purpose flour
1 teaspoon baking powder
½ teaspoon baking soda
1 teaspoon ground cinnamon
Pinch of salt
1 cup sweet potato puree
½ cup vegetable oil
½ cup light brown sugar
¼ cup granulated sugar
2 large eggs, room temperature
1 teaspoon vanilla extract
Cooking spray or vegetable oil for greasing (optional)

Directions

1. Preheat the oven at 350°F (177°C).
2. Line a muffin pan with muffin liners or grease each hole with cooking spray or vegetable oil.
3. In a mixing bowl, mix the flour, baking soda, ground cinnamon, salt, and baking powder
4. In another large bowl, with the help of a spatula mix in the sweet potato puree with oil and stir in the light brown sugar and granulated sugar.
5. Stir in the eggs and mix until combined.
6. Then add the dry ingredients and mix until combined. Be careful not to overmix the batter.
7. Stir in the vanilla extract.
8. Transfer the batter to the muffin pan, filling the liners just ¾ full to allow room for the muffins to rise.

9. Bake in the oven for about 12-15 minutes or until a toothpick inserted in the center comes out clean.
10. Remove from the oven and let the muffins rest in the pan for 5 minutes. Then, transfer to a wire rack to cool down.
11. Serve and enjoy.

Nutrition (per serving)
Calories 177, fat 9.3g, carbs 21.6 g,

Protein 2.4 g, sodium 89 mg

Carrot Zucchini Muffins

Makes 12 | Prep time 15 minutes | Cooking time 30 minutes

Ingredients

1 cup zucchini, grated
1 cup carrots, grated
1 egg beaten
½ teaspoon orange extract
1 cup whole wheat flour
1 teaspoon baking powder
½ teaspoon ground ginger
½ teaspoon cinnamon
3 tablespoons butter, melted and cooled
1 tablespoon honey, or preferred sugar substitute
Cooking spray or vegetable oil for greasing (optional)

Directions

1. Preheat the oven to 325°F (163°C).
2. Line a muffin pan with muffin liners or grease each hole with cooking spray or vegetable oil.
3. Combine the zucchini and carrots in a bowl.
4. Combine the egg, melted butter, honey, and orange extract. Add the mixture to the zucchini and carrots. Mix well.
5. In another large bowl, combine the flour, baking soda, and cinnamon.
6. Add the dry ingredients to the wet ingredients and mix until combined.
7. Transfer the batter to the muffin pan, filling the liners just ¾ full to allow room for the muffins to rise.
8. Bake in the oven for about 12-15 minutes or until a toothpick inserted in the center comes out clean.

9. Remove from the oven and let the muffins rest in the pan for 5 minutes. Then, transfer to a wire rack to cool down.
10. Let cool before eating.

Nutrition (per serving)
Calories 77.8, fat 3.5 g, carbs 10.6 g,
Protein 2.1 g, sodium 53.9 mg

GLUTEN-FREE MUFFINS

Gluten-Free Spice Muffins

Makes 12 | Prep time 10 minutes | Cooking time 20 minutes

Ingredients
3 large eggs, whisked
3 cups flour
½ cup butter, melted
1 teaspoon baking soda
1 teaspoon nutmeg
¼ teaspoon cloves
3 tablespoons cinnamon
¼ cup applesauce
1 teaspoon lemon juice
¼ cup sugar
Cooking spray or vegetable oil for greasing (optional)

Directions

1. Preheat the oven to 350°F (177°C).
2. Line a muffin pan with muffin liners or grease each hole with cooking spray or vegetable oil.
3. Add the dry ingredients to a mixing bowl. Mix well.
4. In another large bowl, beat the eggs. Add the applesauce, butter, and lemon juice. Mix well.
5. Add the dry ingredients to the wet ingredients and mix until combined.
6. Transfer the batter to the muffin pan, filling the liners just ¾ full to allow room for the muffins to rise.
7. Bake in the oven for about 12-15 minutes or until a toothpick inserted in the center comes out clean.

8. Remove from the oven and let the muffins rest in the pan for 5 minutes. Then, transfer to a wire rack to cool down.
9. Gently remove muffins from cups; serve fresh.

Nutrition (per serving)
Calories 273, fat 22 g, carbs 15 g,
Protein 7 g, sodium 52 mg

Gluten-Free Blueberry Muffins

Makes 12 | Prep time 10 minutes | Cooking time 25 minutes

Ingredients
Muffins
3½ cups almond meal
3–4 tablespoons granulated erythritol
2 teaspoons baking powder
6 medium eggs
1¼ cups plain full-fat yogurt
¼ cup butter, melted
2 teaspoons vanilla extract
½ cup fresh wild blueberries
Cooking spray or vegetable oil for greasing (optional)

Topping
¾ cup erythritol
¾ cup almond flour
½ cup cold butter, chopped

Directions

1. Preheat the oven to 350°F (177ºC).
2. Line a muffin pan with muffin liners or grease each hole with cooking spray or vegetable oil.
3. In a bowl, mix the flour, erythritol, and baking powder.
4. In another large bowl, beat the eggs, yogurt, butter, and vanilla until well combined.
5. Add the flour mixture and mix until just combined. Gently fold in the blueberries.
6. For the topping, in a bowl, mix all of the ingredients until a crumbly mixture forms.
7. Transfer the batter mixture into the prepared muffin cups and sprinkle each with a topping mixture.

8. Bake for about 25 minutes or until a toothpick inserted in the center comes out clean.
9. Remove from the oven and let the muffins rest in the pan for 5 minutes. Then, transfer to a wire rack to cool down.
10. Carefully invert the muffins onto the wire rack to cool completely before serving.

Nutrition (per serving)
Calories 398, fat 34 g, carbs 9 g,
Protein 4 g, sodium 129 mg

Gluten-Free Lemon Poppy Seed Muffins

Makes 14 | Prep time 15 minutes | Cooking time 30 minutes

Ingredients

2 cups almond flour
⅓ cup erythritol
1 teaspoon poppy seeds
1 teaspoon baking powder
2 eggs
¼ cup butter, melted
¼ cup sour cream
2 tablespoons lemon juice
1 teaspoon lemon extract
1 teaspoon lemon zest
Cooking spray or vegetable oil for greasing (optional)

Directions

1. Preheat the oven to 350°F (177°C).
2. Line a muffin pan with muffin liners or grease each hole with cooking spray or vegetable oil.
3. In a bowl, mix the flour, erythritol, poppy seeds, and baking powder.
4. Add the remaining ingredients and mix well.
5. Transfer the batter to the muffin pan, filling the liners just ¾ full to allow room for the muffins to rise.
6. Bake in the oven for about 12-15 minutes or until a toothpick inserted in the center comes out clean.
7. Remove from the oven and let the muffins rest in the pan for 5 minutes. Then, transfer to a wire rack to cool down.

Nutrition (per serving)

Calories 150, fat 13.3 g, carbs 3.4 g,
Protein 1 g, sodium 35 mg

Gluten-Free Banana Chocolate Chip Muffins

Makes 12 | Prep time 10 minutes | Cooking time 15 minutes

Ingredients
1 ¼ cups almond flour
¼ cup coconut flour
1 cup light brown sugar
1 ¼ teaspoons baking powder
1 teaspoon ground cinnamon
½ cup vegetable oil
1 large egg, room temperature
2 large bananas, mashed
1 teaspoon vanilla extract
¼ cup coconut or almond milk
¾ cup semi-sweet chocolate chips
Cooking spray or vegetable oil for greasing (optional)

Directions

1. Preheat the oven at 350°F (177°C).
2. Line a muffin pan with muffin liners or grease each hole with cooking spray or vegetable oil.
3. In a mixing bowl, mix the almond flour, coconut flour, cinnamon, and baking powder.
4. In another large bowl, whisk the vegetable oil and light brown sugar until combined. Stir in the eggs. Stir in the mashed bananas.
5. Then alternatively add the whole milk with the dry ingredients and mix until combined. Be careful not to overmix the batter.
6. Stir in the vanilla extract and mix in the chocolate chips.
7. Transfer the batter to the muffin pan, filling the liners just ¾ full to allow room for the muffins to rise.

8. Bake in the oven for about 12-15 minutes or until a toothpick inserted in the center comes out clean.
9. Remove from the oven and let the muffins rest in the pan for 5 minutes. Then, transfer to a wire rack to cool down.
10. Serve and enjoy.

Nutrition (per serving)
Calories 238, fat 17.9 g, carbs 33.6 g,
Protein 2.6 g, sodium 12 mg

Gluten-Free Tutti Fruity Muffins

Makes 18 | Prep time 10 minutes | Cooking time 30 minutes

Ingredients
1 ½ cups sweet potato, mashed
4 eggs
1 ½ cups raw almonds
2 teaspoons baking powder
2 teaspoons cinnamon
1 teaspoon ground ginger
½ teaspoon coriander
1 cup zucchini, shredded
1 cup apple, shredded
1 cup unsweetened shredded coconut
1 cup dried apricots, chopped
½ cup dates, chopped
1 cup walnuts, chopped
Cooking spray or vegetable oil for greasing (optional)

Directions

1. Preheat the oven to 375°F (190°C).
2. Line a muffin pan with muffin liners or grease each hole with cooking spray or vegetable oil.
3. Place almonds in a food processor and grind finely.
4. In a bowl, combine the sweet potatoes with the eggs, almond flour, baking powder, cinnamon, ginger, and coriander. Mix just until blended.
5. Next, fold in the zucchini, apple, coconut, apricots, dates, and walnuts.
6. Transfer the batter to the muffin pan, filling the liners just ¾ full to allow room for the muffins to rise.

7. Bake in the oven for about 12-15 minutes or until a toothpick inserted in the center comes out clean.
8. Remove from the oven and let the muffins rest in the pan for 5 minutes. Then, transfer to a wire rack to cool down.
9. Remove from the oven and let cool slightly before serving.

Nutrition (per serving)

Calories 179, fat 11.7 g, carbs 16.6 g, Protein 5.1 g, sodium 406 mg

Gluten-Free Chocolate Muffins

Makes 12 | Prep time 10 minutes | Cooking time 20 minutes

Ingredients
½ cup granulated erythritol
1½ teaspoons baking powder
1 cup almond flour
½ cup unsweetened cocoa powder
1 teaspoon vanilla extract
3 large eggs
⅔ cup heavy cream
3 ounces unsalted butter, melted
½ cup unsweetened chocolate chips
Cooking spray or vegetable oil for greasing (optional)

Directions

1. Preheat the oven to 350°F (177°C).
2. Line a muffin pan with muffin liners or grease each hole with cooking spray or vegetable oil.
3. Add the cocoa powder, almond flour, erythritol, and baking powder to a mixing bowl.
4. Add the eggs, vanilla extract, and heavy cream. Mix well until no visible lumps remain.
5. Add the melted butter and continue to mix. Add the chocolate chips and mix again.
6. Transfer the batter to the muffin pan, filling the liners just ¾ full to allow room for the muffins to rise.
7. Bake for 20 minutes until a toothpick inserted in the center comes out clean.
8. Remove from the oven and let the muffins rest in the pan for 5 minutes. Then, transfer to a wire rack to cool down.
9. Gently take the muffins out of the cups; serve fresh.

Nutrition (per serving)
Calories 212, fat 20 g, carbs 8 g,
Protein 5 g, sodium 27 mg

Gluten-Free Blueberry Muffins

Makes 12 | Prep time 20 minutes | Cooking time 25 minutes

Ingredients
1 tablespoon baking powder
1 teaspoon salt
1 teaspoon baking soda
3 cups almond flour
¼ cup coconut flour
7 tablespoons coconut oil
¾ cup granulated sweetener
½ cup applesauce, unsweetened
2 teaspoons vanilla extract
3 large eggs
⅔ cup fresh blueberries
Cooking spray or vegetable oil for greasing (optional)

Directions

1. Preheat the oven to 350°F (177°C). Line a muffin pan with muffin liners or grease each hole with cooking spray or vegetable oil.
2. Add the coconut flour, almond flour, baking powder, salt, and baking soda to a mixing bowl. Mix well.
3. In another large bowl, beat the eggs. Add the sweetener, applesauce, coconut oil, and vanilla. Mix well.
4. Combine the mixtures and mix well until no visible lumps remain.
5. Mix in the blueberries and set aside for 5 minutes.
6. Bake for 23–25 minutes until the muffins turn a toothpick inserted in the center comes out clean.
7. Remove from the oven and let the muffins rest in the pan for 5 minutes. Then, transfer to a wire rack to cool down.

8. Gently take the muffins out of the cups; serve fresh.

Nutrition (per serving)
Calories 247, fat 22 g, carbs 9.5 g,
Protein 7.5 g, sodium 218 mg

Gluten-Free Banana Walnut Muffins

Makes 10 | Prep time 10 minutes | Cooking time 20 minutes

Ingredients
2 tablespoons ground flaxseed (optional)
2 teaspoons baking powder
1¼ cups almond flour
½ cup powdered erythritol
5 tablespoons butter, melted
½ teaspoons ground cinnamon
2½ teaspoons banana extract
1 teaspoon vanilla extract
¼ cup sour cream
¼ cup almond milk, unsweetened
2 eggs
Cooking spray or vegetable oil for greasing (optional)

Topping
¾ cup chopped walnuts
1 tablespoon almond flour
1 tablespoon butter, cold
1 tablespoon powdered erythritol

Directions

1. Preheat the oven to 350°F (177°C).
2. Line a muffin pan with muffin liners or grease each hole with cooking spray or vegetable oil.
3. Add the almond flour, baking powder, ground flaxseed, cinnamon, and erythritol to a mixing bowl. Mix well.
4. Add the vanilla extract, butter, banana extract, almond milk, and sour cream.
5. Mix well. Add the eggs and mix well until no visible lumps remain.

6. Transfer the batter to the muffin pan, filling the liners just ¾ full to allow room for the muffins to rise.
7. In a food processor, chop the walnuts, butter, and almond flour into small pieces. Add more butter if the mixture is too dry.
8. Sprinkle the nut mixture over the batter evenly and press down gently. Sprinkle powdered erythritol on top.
9. Bake for 20 minutes until a toothpick inserted in the center comes out clean.
10. Remove from the oven and let the muffins rest in the pan for 5 minutes. Then, transfer to a wire rack to cool down.

Nutrition (per serving)
Calories 248, fat 22 g, carbs 7 g,
Protein 7 g, sodium 91 mg

Gluten-Free Poppy Seed Lemon Muffins

Makes 12 | Prep time 10 minutes | Cooking time 20 minutes

Ingredients
⅓ cup erythritol
1 teaspoon baking powder
¾ cup almond flour
¼ cup golden flaxseed meal
2 tablespoons poppy seeds
¼ cup heavy cream
¼ cup salted butter, melted
3 large eggs
3 tablespoons lemon juice
Zest of 2 lemons
1 teaspoon vanilla extract
25 drops liquid stevia
Cooking spray or vegetable oil for greasing (optional)

Directions

1. Preheat the oven to 350°F (177°C).
2. Line a muffin pan with muffin liners or grease each hole with cooking spray or vegetable oil.
3. Add the almond flour, flaxseed meal, poppy seeds, and erythritol to a mixing bowl. Mix well.
4. Add the eggs, butter, and heavy cream. Mix well until no visible lumps remain.
5. Mix in the vanilla extract, baking powder, liquid stevia, lemon zest, and lemon juice.
6. Transfer the batter to the muffin pan, filling the liners just ¾ full to allow room for the muffins to rise.
7. Bake for 18–20 minutes until the muffins turn a toothpick inserted in the center comes out clean.

8. Remove from the oven and let the muffins rest in the pan for 5 minutes. Then, transfer to a wire rack to cool down.
9. Gently remove muffins from cups; serve fresh.

Nutrition (per serving)
Calories 129, fat 11.5 g, carbs 3.5 g,
Protein 4 g, sodium 142 mg

Gluten-Free Vanilla Muffins

Makes 12 | Prep time 10 minutes | Cooking time 20 minutes

Ingredients
2 ounces cream cheese, softened
2 tablespoons butter, softened
⅓ cup granular sweetener
½ cup unsweetened vanilla almond milk
4 eggs
2 teaspoons vanilla
1 cup almond flour
½ cup coconut flour
¼ teaspoon salt
1 teaspoon baking powder
Cooking spray or vegetable oil for greasing (optional)

Topping
2 tablespoons coconut flour
1 cup almond flour
¼ cup granular sweetener
¼ cup butter, softened
1 teaspoon cinnamon
½ teaspoon molasses (optional)

Directions

1. Preheat the oven to 350°F (177°C).
2. Line a muffin pan with muffin liners or grease each hole with cooking spray or vegetable oil.
3. Add the batter ingredients to a blender or food processor and blend until well combined.
4. Transfer the batter to the muffin pan, filling the liners just ¾ full to allow room for the muffins to rise.

5. Add the topping ingredients to a blender or food processor and blend until crumbs form.
6. Sprinkle the topping over the batter in the muffin cups.
7. Bake for 20–25 minutes until the muffins turn a toothpick inserted in the center comes out clean.
8. Remove from the oven and let the muffins rest in the pan for 5 minutes. Then, transfer to a wire rack to cool down.
9. Gently remove muffins from cups; serve fresh.

Nutrition (per serving)
Calories 222, fat 18 g, carbs 9 g,
Protein 7 g, sodium 156 mg

Gluten-Free Pumpkin Cinnamon Muffins

Makes 20 | Prep time 10 minutes | Cooking time 15 minutes

Ingredients
1 tablespoon cinnamon
½ cup almond flour
1 teaspoon baking powder
½ cup nut butter (almond, peanut, etc.)
½ cup coconut oil
½ cup pumpkin puree
Cooking spray or vegetable oil for greasing (optional)

<u>Glaze</u>
¼ cup almond or coconut milk
¼ cup coconut butter
1 tablespoon granulated sweetener
2 teaspoons lemon juice

Directions

1. Preheat the oven to 350°F (177°C).
2. Line a muffin pan with muffin liners or grease each hole with cooking spray or vegetable oil.
3. Add the dry ingredients to a mixing bowl. Mix well.
4. In another bowl, add the butter, coconut oil, and pumpkin puree. Mix well.
5. Combine the mixtures and mix well until no visible lumps remain.
6. Transfer the batter to the muffin pan, filling the liners just ¾ full to allow room for the muffins to rise.
7. Bake for 10–15 minutes until the muffins turn a toothpick inserted in the center comes out clean.
8. Remove from the oven and let the muffins rest in the pan for 5 minutes. Then, transfer to a wire rack to cool down.

9. In another large bowl combine all of the glaze ingredients.
10. Gently remove muffins from cups. Drizzle with glaze. Set aside until they firm up. Serve fresh.

Nutrition (per serving)

Calories 112, fat 9 g, carbs 3 g,
Protein 5 g, sodium 64 mg

Gluten-Free Raspberry Muffins

Makes 10 | Prep time 10 minutes | Cooking time 25 minutes

Ingredients
2½ cups blanched almond flour, finely ground and sifted
⅓ cup granulated sweetener
¼ teaspoon salt
1½ teaspoons baking powder
⅓ cup unsweetened almond or cashew milk
⅓ cup coconut oil or melted butter
½ teaspoon vanilla extract
3 large eggs
¾ cup raspberries, fresh or frozen and thawed
Cooking spray or vegetable oil for greasing (optional)

Directions

1. Preheat the oven to 350°F (175°C).
2. Line a muffin pan with muffin liners or grease each hole with cooking spray or vegetable oil.
3. Add the granulated sweetener, almond flour, baking powder, and salt to a mixing bowl. Mix well.
4. Mix in the berries. In another large bowl, beat the eggs. Add the vanilla extract, coconut oil or butter, and almond milk. Mix well.
5. Combine the mixtures and mix well until no visible lumps remain.
6. Transfer the batter to the muffin pan, filling the liners just ¾ full to allow room for the muffins to rise.
7. Bake for 25 minutes until the muffins turn a toothpick inserted in the center comes out clean.
8. Remove from the oven and let the muffins rest in the pan for 5 minutes. Then, transfer to a wire rack to cool down.

9.   Gently remove muffins from cups; serve fresh.

Nutrition (per serving)
Calories 277, fat 25 g, carbs 8 g,
Protein 8 g, sodium 101 mg

Gluten-Free Apple Spice Muffins

Makes 12 | Prep time 10 minutes | Cooking time 25 minutes

Ingredients
1 teaspoon baking powder
1 teaspoon ground cinnamon
½ teaspoon salt
2½ cups almond flour
¾ cup granulated stevia or erythritol
4 large eggs
¼ cup butter or coconut oil, melted
¼ cup unsweetened almond milk
1 teaspoon vanilla extract
1 small (4 ounces) Granny Smith apple, peeled, seeded, and finely diced
Cooking spray or vegetable oil for greasing (optional)

Directions

1. Preheat the oven to 350°F (177°C).
2. Line a muffin pan with muffin liners or grease each hole with cooking spray or vegetable oil.
3. Add the almond flour, baking powder, sweetener, cinnamon, and salt to a mixing bowl. Mix well.
4. Add the butter or coconut oil. Mix again.
5. In another large bowl, beat the eggs. Add the almond milk and vanilla. Mix well.
6. Combine the mixtures and mix well until no visible lumps remain. Mix in the diced apple.
7. Transfer the batter to the muffin pan, filling the liners just ¾ full to allow room for the muffins to rise.
8. Bake for 25–30 minutes until the muffins turn a toothpick inserted in the center comes out clean.

9. Remove from the oven and let the muffins rest in the pan for 5 minutes. Then, transfer to a wire rack to cool down.
10. Gently remove muffins from cups; serve fresh.

Nutrition (per serving)
Calories 198, fat 17 g, carbs 7 g,
Protein 7 g, sodium 185 mg

Gluten-Free Carrot Cake Muffins

Makes 12 | Prep time 10 minutes | Cooking time 45 minutes

Ingredients
1 teaspoon baking powder
1 teaspoon cinnamon
1 cup almond flour
½ cup granular sweetener
½ teaspoon salt
3 small carrots, shredded
¾ cup olive oil
2 eggs, beaten
Cooking spray or vegetable oil for greasing (optional)

Frosting
2 tablespoons butter, room temperature
4 ounces cream cheese, room temperature
¼ cup powdered sweetener
½ teaspoon vanilla extract
¼ teaspoon almond extract
2 tablespoons heavy whipping cream
4 drops liquid stevia

Directions

1. Preheat the oven to 350°F (177°C).
2. Line a muffin pan with muffin liners or grease each hole with cooking spray or vegetable oil.
3. Add the almond flour, baking powder, sweetener, cinnamon, and salt to a mixing bowl. Mix well.
4. In another large bowl beat the eggs. Add the carrots and olive oil. Mix well.
5. Combine the mixtures and mix well until no visible lumps remain.

6. Transfer the batter to the muffin pan, filling the liners just ¾ full to allow room for the muffins to rise.
7. Bake for 40–45 minutes until the muffins turn a toothpick inserted in the center comes out clean.
8. Remove from the oven and let the muffins rest in the pan for 5 minutes. Then, transfer to a wire rack to cool down.
9. Gently remove muffins from cups. Set aside.
10. To make the frosting, add the butter and cream cheese to a mixing bowl. Mix well.
11. Add the heavy cream, sweetener, vanilla, almond, and stevia, and mix well.
12. Pour the frosting over the muffins. Serve fresh or refrigerate until frosting has firmed up.

Nutrition (per serving)
Calories 251, fat 25 g, carbs 5 g,
Protein 4 g, sodium 196 mg

Gluten-Free Pumpkin Cheese Muffins

Makes 12 | Prep time 10 minutes | Cooking time 20 minutes

Ingredients
4 large eggs
½ cup butter, softened
⅔ cup + 1 tablespoon granulated erythritol
¾ cup pumpkin puree
1 teaspoon vanilla extract
4 teaspoons baking powder
2 teaspoons pumpkin spice
1½ cups almond flour
½ cup coconut flour
½ teaspoon salt
8 ounces cream cheese, softened
Cooking spray or vegetable oil for greasing (optional)

Directions

1. Preheat the oven to 350°F (177°C).
2. Line a muffin pan with muffin liners or grease each hole with cooking spray or vegetable oil.
3. Add the butter and ⅔ cup erythritol to a mixing bowl. Mix until fluffy.
4. In another large bowl, beat the eggs. Add the butter mixture, pumpkin puree, and vanilla. Mix well.
5. Add the baking powder, almond flour, coconut flour, pumpkin spice, and salt to a mixing bowl. Mix well.
6. Combine the mixtures and mix well until no visible lumps remain.
7. Transfer the batter to the muffin pan, filling the liners just ¾ full to allow room for the muffins to rise.

8. Add the 1 tablespoon erythritol and softened cream cheese to a mixing bowl. Mix well.
9. Drop a spoonful of the mixture over each muffin and spread evenly.
10. Bake for 20–25 minutes until the muffins turn a toothpick inserted in the center comes out clean.
11. Remove from the oven and let the muffins rest in the pan for 5 minutes. Then, transfer to a wire rack to cool down.
12. Gently remove muffins from cups; serve fresh.

Nutrition (per serving)
Calories 261, fat 23 g, carbs 6 g,
Protein 7 g, sodium 623 mg

Gluten-Free Zucchini Spice Muffins

Makes 8 | Prep time 10 minutes | Cooking time 25 minutes

Ingredients
1 cup grated zucchini
⅓ cup coconut oil
6 medium eggs
¾ cup coconut flour
¼ cup granulated sweetener
½ teaspoon baking soda
1 teaspoon cinnamon
¼ teaspoon nutmeg, grated
4 drops stevia liquid
Cooking spray or vegetable oil for greasing (optional)

Directions

1. Preheat the oven to 350°F (177°C).
2. Line a muffin pan with muffin liners or grease each hole with cooking spray or vegetable oil.
3. Heat the oil over medium heat in a medium saucepan or skillet.
4. Add the zucchini and stir-cook until well mixed with the oil.
5. Add all the ingredients except for the zucchini to a mixing bowl. Mix well.
6. Add the cooked zucchini.
7. Mix well until no visible lumps remain.
8. Transfer the batter to the muffin pan, filling the liners just ¾ full to allow room for the muffins to rise.
9. Bake for 25 minutes until the muffins turn a toothpick inserted in the center comes out clean.

10. Remove from the oven and let the muffins rest in the pan for 5 minutes. Then, transfer to a wire rack to cool down.
11. Gently remove muffins from cups; serve fresh.

Nutrition (per serving)
Calories 175, fat 13 g, carbs 6.5 g,
Protein 5.5 g, sodium 68 mg

Gluten-Free Strawberry Muffins

Makes 12 | Prep time 10 minutes | Cooking time 20 minutes

Ingredients
⅓ cup unsweetened vanilla almond milk
3 large eggs
½ cup granular erythritol
⅓ cup coconut oil
2½ cups almond flour
2 teaspoons baking powder
1 cup strawberries, fresh or thawed
Cooking spray or vegetable oil for greasing (optional)

Directions

1. Preheat the oven to 350°F (177°C).
2. Line a muffin pan with muffin liners or grease each hole with cooking spray or vegetable oil.
3. Add the baking powder and almond flour to a mixing bowl. Mix well.
4. In another large bowl, whisk the eggs. Add the almond milk, sweetener, and coconut oil. Mix well.
5. Combine the mixtures and mix well until no visible lumps remain. Mix in the strawberries.
6. Transfer the batter to the muffin pan, filling the liners just ¾ full to allow room for the muffins to rise.
7. Bake for 22–25 minutes until the muffins turn a toothpick inserted in the center comes out clean.
8. Remove from the oven and let the muffins rest in the pan for 5 minutes. Then, transfer to a wire rack to cool down.
9. Gently remove muffins from cups; serve fresh.

Nutrition (per serving)
Calories 207, fat 19 g, carbs 6.5 g,

Protein 6.5 g, sodium 97 mg

Gluten-Free Applesauce Muffins

Makes 12 | Prep time 10 minutes | Cooking time 20 minutes

Ingredients

3 large eggs, whisked
3 cups almond flour
½ cup ghee, melted
1 teaspoon baking soda
1 teaspoon nutmeg
¼ teaspoon cloves
3 tablespoons cinnamon
¼ cup applesauce
1 teaspoon lemon juice
Stevia to taste
Cooking spray or vegetable oil for greasing (optional)

Directions

1. Preheat the oven to 350°F (177°C).
2. Line a muffin pan with muffin liners or grease each hole with cooking spray or vegetable oil.
3. Add the dry ingredients to a mixing bowl. Mix well.
4. In another large bowl, beat the eggs. Add the applesauce, ghee, and lemon juice. Mix well.
5. Combine the mixtures and mix well until no visible lumps remain.
6. Transfer the batter to the muffin pan, filling the liners just ¾ full to allow room for the muffins to rise.
7. Bake for 18–20 minutes until the muffins turn a toothpick inserted in the center comes out clean.
8. Remove from the oven and let the muffins rest in the pan for 5 minutes. Then, transfer to a wire rack to cool down.
9. Gently remove muffins from cups; serve fresh.

Nutrition (per serving)
Calories 241, fat 22 g, carbs 7 g,
Protein 7 g, sodium 52 mg

Gluten-Free Creamy Chocolate Muffins

Makes 10 | Prep time 15 minutes | Cooking time 25 minutes

Ingredients
<u>Dry Ingredients</u>
1 cup almond flour
⅓ cup coconut flour
½ cup granular sweetener
1 teaspoon cinnamon
1 teaspoon baking soda
2 teaspoons cream of tartar
⅓ cup unsweetened cocoa powder
⅓ cup dark chocolate, roughly chopped
Cooking spray or vegetable oil for greasing (optional)

<u>Wet Ingredients</u>
4 large eggs
2 tablespoons coconut milk or heavy cream
2 medium avocados, peeled, seeded, and halved
15–20 drops stevia liquid

Directions

1. Preheat the oven to 350°F (177°C).
2. Line a muffin pan with muffin liners or grease each hole with cooking spray or vegetable oil.
3. Add the avocado halves to a blender or food processor until smooth.
4. Add the other wet ingredients and blend until smooth.
5. Add the dry ingredients except for the chocolate to a mixing bowl. Mix well.
6. Add the avocado mixture. Mix well until no visible lumps remain.
7. Mix in the chocolate pieces, reserving some for topping.

8. Transfer the batter to the muffin pan, filling the liners just ¾ full to allow room for the muffins to rise.
9. Bake in the oven for about 12-15 minutes or until a toothpick inserted in the center comes out clean.
10. Remove from the oven and let the muffins rest in the pan for 5 minutes. Then, transfer to a wire rack to cool down.

Nutrition (per serving)
Calories 210, fat 16 g, carbs 13.5 g,
Protein 7.5 g, sodium 169 mg

Gluten-Free Zucchini Chocolate Muffins

Makes 12 | Prep time 10 minutes | Cooking time 25 minutes

Ingredients
¼ teaspoon salt
½ teaspoon baking soda
2 cups almond flour (or almond meal)
¼ cup unsweetened cocoa
¼ cup coconut oil
¼ cup granular sweetener
3 large eggs
½ cup sugar-free dark chocolate chips (optional)
¾ cup shredded zucchini
Cooking spray or vegetable oil for greasing (optional)

Directions

1. Preheat the oven to 350°F (177°C).
2. Line a muffin pan with muffin liners or grease each hole with cooking spray or vegetable oil.
3. Add the almond flour, salt, cocoa, and baking soda to a mixing bowl. Mix well.
4. In another large bowl, beat the eggs. Add the sweetener and coconut oil. Mix well.
5. Mix in the zucchini and chocolate chips.
6. Combine the mixtures and mix well until no visible lumps remain.
7. Transfer the batter to the muffin pan, filling the liners just ¾ full to allow room for the muffins to rise.
8. Bake for 22–25 minutes until the muffins turn a toothpick inserted in the center comes out clean.
9. Remove from the oven and let the muffins rest in the pan for 5 minutes. Then, transfer to a wire rack to cool down.

Nutrition (per serving)
Calories 247, fat 16 g, carbs 14 g,
Protein 6 g, sodium 117 mg

Gluten-Free Orange Muffins

Makes 6 | Prep time 10 minutes | Cooking time 30 minutes

Ingredients
2 tablespoons coconut oil
¼ cup fresh orange juice
2 cups almond flour, blanched
3 large eggs
½ teaspoon cardamom
1 teaspoon baking powder
¼ teaspoon sea salt
1 tablespoon orange zest
2 teaspoons stevia powder
Cooking spray or vegetable oil for greasing (optional)

Glaze
1 tablespoon coconut oil
½ tablespoon stevia powder
¼ cup coconut butter

Directions

1. For the glaze, melt the butter in a saucepan; add the coconut oil and stir until smooth.
2. Remove from heat; mix in the stevia powder. Set aside.
3. Preheat the oven to 350°F (177°C).
4. Line a muffin pan with muffin liners or grease each hole with cooking spray or vegetable oil.
5. Whisk the eggs in a bowl. Add the orange juice and orange zest. Mix well.
6. Add the baking powder, cardamom, almond flour, stevia, and salt to a mixing bowl. Mix well.
7. Combine the mixtures and mix well. Add the coconut oil.
8. Mix well until no visible lumps remain.

9. Transfer the batter to the muffin pan, filling the liners just ¾ full to allow room for the muffins to rise.
10. Bake for 25–30 minutes until the muffins turn a toothpick inserted in the center comes out clean.
11. Remove from the oven and let the muffins rest in the pan for 5 minutes. Then, transfer to a wire rack to cool down.
12. Gently remove muffins from cups; drizzle with prepared glaze and serve fresh.

Nutrition (per serving)
Calories 257, fat 26 g, carbs 11 g,
Protein 12.5 g, sodium 218 mg

Gluten-Free Peanut Butter Chocolate Muffins

Makes 6 | Prep time 20 minutes | Cooking time 25 minutes

Ingredients
1 teaspoon baking powder
1 pinch salt
1 cup almond flour
½ cup granular sweetener
⅓ cup low-carb unsweetened peanut butter
2 large eggs
⅓ cup almond milk
½ cup cacao nibs or unsweetened chocolate chips
Cooking spray or vegetable oil for greasing (optional)

Directions

1. Preheat the oven to 350°F (177°C).
2. Line a muffin pan with muffin liners or grease each hole with cooking spray or vegetable oil.
3. Add the almond flour, salt, baking powder, and sweetener to a mixing bowl. Mix well.
4. In another large bowl, beat the eggs. Add the peanut butter and almond milk. Mix well.
5. Combine the mixtures and mix well until no visible lumps remain.
6. Mix in the cacao nibs.
7. Transfer the batter to the muffin pan, filling the liners just ¾ full to allow room for the muffins to rise.
8. Bake for 25–30 minutes until the muffins turn a toothpick inserted in the center comes out clean.
9. Remove from the oven and let the muffins rest in the pan for 5 minutes. Then, transfer to a wire rack to cool down.
10. Gently remove muffins from cups; serve fresh.

Nutrition (per serving)
Calories 265, fat 20.5 g, carbs 4.5 g,
Protein 7.5 g, sodium 210 mg

SAVORY MUFFINS

Zucchini Bacon Muffins

Makes 8 | Prep time 15 minutes | Cooking time 30 minutes

Ingredients

2 sprigs fresh thyme
½ cup flour
2 cups grated zucchini
1 green onion, chopped
7 large eggs
4–5 slices bacon, diced
½ teaspoon salt
1 teaspoon ground turmeric
½ tablespoon vinegar
1 teaspoon baking powder

Directions

1. Add the bacon to a medium saucepan or skillet and cook over medium heat until evenly crisp and brown. Drain over paper towels.
2. Preheat the oven to 350°F (177°C). Line an 8-cup muffin pan with parchment paper liners or grease with vegetable oil or cooking spray.
3. Add the bacon pieces and other dry ingredients to a mixing bowl. Mix well.
4. In another large bowl, beat the eggs. Add the vinegar. Mix well.
5. Combine the mixtures and mix well until no visible lumps remain.
6. Transfer the batter to the muffin pan, filling the liners just ¾ full to allow room for the muffins to rise.

7. Bake for 30 minutes until the muffins turn a toothpick inserted in the center comes out clean.
8. Remove from the oven and let the muffins rest in the pan for 5 minutes. Then, transfer to a wire rack to cool down.
9. Gently remove muffins from cups; serve fresh.

Nutrition (per serving)
Calories 104, fat 7 g, carbs 2.5 g,
Protein 8 g, sodium 388 mg

Zucchini Ham Muffins

Makes 12 | Prep time 10 minutes | Cooking time 35 minutes

Ingredients
4 eggs
⅓ cup sour cream
1 zucchini, grated
3½ ounces Parmesan cheese, grated
5 ounces ham, diced
1 teaspoon baking powder
½ teaspoon salt
½ teaspoon pepper
1 cup all-purpose flour

Directions

1. Preheat the oven to 350°F (177°C). Line a 12-cup muffin pan with parchment paper liners.
2. Add the cheese, ham, zucchini, eggs, and sour cream to a mixing bowl. Mix well.
3. To another mixing bowl, add the baking powder, all-purpose flour, salt, and pepper. Mix well.
4. Combine the mixtures and mix well until no visible lumps remain.
5. Transfer the batter to the muffin pan, filling the liners just ¾ full to allow room for the muffins to rise.
6. Bake for 30 minutes or until a toothpick inserted in the center comes out clean.
7. Remove from the oven and let the muffins rest in the pan for 5 minutes. Then, transfer to a wire rack to cool down.
8. Gently remove muffins from cups; serve fresh.

Nutrition (per serving)

Calories 135, fat 9 g, carbs 3 g,
Protein 9 g, sodium 420 mg

Egg and Broccoli Muffins

Makes 12 | Prep time 10 minutes | Cooking time 20 minutes

Ingredients

¼ cup heavy whipping cream
1 cup cheddar cheese, shredded
1½ cups broccoli florets
10 large eggs
2 scallions, green and white parts, thinly sliced
¼ teaspoon pepper
1 tablespoon fresh parsley, minced
1 teaspoon onion powder
1 teaspoon salt

Directions

1. Add the broccoli to boiling water in a saucepan and boil for 90 seconds; drain and set aside.
2. Preheat the oven to 400°F (204°C). Grease a 12-cup muffin pan with coconut/avocado oil or cooking spray.
3. In another large bowl, beat the eggs and cream. Add the scallions, cheddar, onion powder, salt, and pepper. Mix well.
4. Mix in the broccoli florets and parsley.
5. Transfer the batter to the muffin pan, filling the liners just ¾ full to allow room for the muffins to rise.
6. Bake for 15–20 minutes until the eggs are well set.
7. Remove from the oven and let the muffins rest in the pan for 5 minutes. Then, transfer to a wire rack to cool down.
8. Gently remove muffins from cups; serve fresh.

Nutrition (per serving)

Calories 112, fat 8 g, carbs 1 g,

Protein 7 g, sodium 310 mg

Broccoli Cheese Muffins

Makes 12 | Prep time 10 minutes | Cooking time 15 minutes

Ingredients

½ teaspoon dried thyme
½ teaspoon garlic powder
10 large eggs
1–1½ teaspoons salt or to taste
¼–½ teaspoon pepper or to taste
⅔ cup grated Swiss cheese or Cheddar cheese
1½ cups broccoli, steamed and chopped

Directions

1. Preheat the oven to 400°F (204°C). Line a 12-cup muffin pan with silicone liners or grease with coconut/olive oil or cooking spray.
2. In another large bowl, beat the eggs. Add the salt and pepper. Mix well.
3. Add the garlic powder and thyme; mix well.
4. Mix in the broccoli and cheese.
5. Evenly distribute the batter among the muffin cups until they are about ⅔ full. Add more cheese on top, if desired.
6. Bake for 12–15 minutes until well set.
7. Remove from the oven and let the muffins rest in the pan for 5 minutes. Then, transfer to a wire rack to cool down.
8. Gently take the muffins out of the cups; serve fresh.

Nutrition (per serving)

Calories 82, fat 5 g, carbs 1 g,
Protein 6 g, sodium 94 mg

Spinach Egg Muffins

Makes 12 | Prep time 10 minutes | Cooking time 15 minutes

Ingredients
10 large eggs
½ teaspoon garlic powder
½ teaspoon dried basil
1–1½ teaspoons salt or to taste
¼–½ teaspoon pepper or to taste
2 cups spinach, chopped
1½ cups grated Parmesan cheese

Directions

1. Preheat the oven to 400°F (204°C). Line a 12-cup muffin pan with paper liners or grease with coconut/olive oil or cooking spray.
2. In another large bowl, beat the eggs. Add the salt and pepper. Mix well.
3. Add the garlic powder and basil; mix well.
4. Add the cheese and spinach; mix again.
5. Transfer the batter to the muffin pan, filling the liners just ¾ full to allow room for the muffins to rise.
6. Bake for 12–15 minutes until the eggs are well set.
7. Remove from the oven and let the muffins rest in the pan for 5 minutes. Then, transfer to a wire rack to cool down.
8. Gently remove muffins from cups; serve fresh.

Nutrition (per serving)
Calories 107, fat 7 g, carbs 1 g,
Protein 9 g, sodium 277 mg

Spinach and Bacon Muffins

Makes 12 | Prep time 15 minutes | Cooking time 35 minutes

Ingredients
1 tablespoon olive oil
1 cup red onion, diced
1 cup fresh spinach, torn
½ cup low sodium bacon, cooked and crumbled
2 teaspoons crushed red pepper flakes
1 ¼ cup whole wheat flour
2 teaspoons baking powder
2 eggs, beaten
1 ½ cup low-fat milk
1 cup feta cheese, crumbled
½ cup fresh grated Parmesan cheese

Directions

1. Preheat oven to 325°F (163°C) and lightly oil a muffin pan.
2. Add the olive oil to a sauté pan and heat over medium. Add the onion and sauté for 2-3 minutes. Add the spinach, bacon, and crushed red pepper. Sauté until spinach is wilted, approximately 1 minute.
3. In a bowl, combine the wheat flour and baking soda.
4. In another large bowl, combine the eggs, milk, feta cheese, and Parmesan cheese.
5. Incorporate the dry ingredients into the wet and then fold in the spinach.
6. Spoon the mixture into muffin pans.
7. Place the muffin pans into the oven and bake for 35 minutes or until golden.

8. Remove from the oven and let the muffins rest in the pan for 5 minutes. Then, transfer to a wire rack to cool down.

Nutrition (per serving)
Calories 92.3, fat 4.4 g, carbs 8.6 g
Protein 5.2 g, sodium 226.4 mg

Spinach Bacon Mushroom Muffins

Makes 12 | Prep time 15 minutes | Cooking time 20 minutes

Ingredients
2 tablespoons finely chopped onion
12 large eggs
Salt and pepper to taste

Spinach
8 grape or cherry tomatoes, halved
¼ cup mozzarella cheese, shredded
¼ cup fresh spinach, roughly chopped

Bacon
¼ cup cheddar cheese, shredded
¼ cup cooked bacon, chopped

Mushrooms
¼ cup red bell pepper, diced
1 tablespoon fresh parsley, chopped
¼ teaspoon garlic powder or ⅓ teaspoon minced garlic
¼ cup brown mushrooms, sliced

Directions

1. Preheat the oven to 350°F (177°C). Grease a 12-cup muffin pan with coconut/olive oil or cooking spray.
2. Beat the eggs in a mixing bowl. Add the onion, salt, and pepper. Mix well.
3. Evenly distribute the batter among the muffin cups until they are about half full.
4. Evenly distribute each topping combination over 4 muffins.
5. Bake for 20 minutes until well set.

6. Remove from the oven and let the muffins rest in the pan for 5 minutes. Then, transfer to a wire rack to cool down.
7. Gently remove muffins from cups; serve fresh.

Nutrition (per serving)
Calories 82, fat 5 g, carbs 1 g,
Protein 6 g, sodium 97 mg

Savory Mushroom Breakfast Muffins

Makes 10 | Prep time 15 minutes | Cooking time 20 minutes

Ingredients
1 cup mushrooms, chopped
2 cloves garlic, crushed and minced
2 ½ cups almond flour
1 teaspoon baking soda
1 tablespoon fresh thyme, chopped
1 teaspoon sea salt
1 teaspoon coarse ground black pepper
3 eggs
⅓ cup cooked sweet potato, mashed
2 tablespoons olive oil
½ cup walnuts, chopped
½ cup brie, cubed

Directions

1. Preheat the oven to 350°F (177°C) and line with paper liners or oil and flour 10 standard-sized muffin cups.
2. Spray a skillet with cooking oil and place it over medium heat.
3. Add the mushrooms and garlic to the skillet and sauté for 2-3 minutes, or until the mushrooms are tender. Remove the skillet from the heat and set it aside.
4. In a bowl, combine the almond flour, baking soda, thyme, sea salt, and black pepper. Mix well.
5. In a separate bowl, combine the eggs, sweet potato, and olive oil. Mix well.
6. Add the dry ingredients to the wet ingredients and blend until just combined.
7. Fold in the mushrooms, walnuts, and brie.

8. Spoon the batter into the prepared muffin cups.
9. Bake for approximately 20 minutes, or until the set in the center.
10. Remove from the oven and let the muffins rest in the pan for 5 minutes. Then, transfer to a wire rack to cool down.

Nutrition (per serving)
Calories 253, fat 22 g, carbs 7.7 g,
Protein 9.7 g, sodium 521 mg

Cornbread Muffins

Makes 12 | Prep time 10 minutes | Cooking time 30 minutes

Ingredients

1½ cups cornmeal
1 cup all-purpose flour
3 teaspoons baking powder
1 ½ teaspoons baking soda
1 teaspoon salt
1 cup grated provolone cheese
2 cups cream
2 large eggs
1 small jalapenos pepper, trimmed, membrane removed, and diced thin
½ cup melted butter
Butter for serving

Directions

1. Preheat the oven to 400°F (204°C).
2. Line a muffin pan with paper liners, and set aside.
3. Add the cornmeal, flour, baking powder, soda, and salt to a large mixing bowl.
4. Stir in the provolone cheese, cream, eggs, jalapenos pepper, and melted butter.
5. Mix until well combined and the batter is smooth.
6. Spoon the batter into the prepared muffin cups. Fill just each muffin cup ¾ of the way full, leaving some space for the muffins to rise.
7. Bake in the oven for about 20 minutes or until a toothpick inserted in the center comes out clean.
8. Remove from the oven and let the muffins rest in the pan for 5 minutes. Then, transfer to a wire rack to cool down.

Nutrition (per serving)
Calories 358, fat 21.5 g, carbs 32.7 g,
Protein 9.9 g, sodium 723 mg

Avocado Bacon Muffins

Makes 16 | Prep time 10 minutes | Cooking time 25 minutes

Ingredients
2 tablespoons butter, melted
1 cup whole-wheat flour
5 large eggs
5 slices bacon
2 medium avocados, pitted and halved
4½ ounces Colby Jack cheese, shredded
1 teaspoon dried cilantro
1 teaspoon dried chives
1 teaspoon minced garlic
¼ teaspoon red chili flakes
3 medium spring onions, chopped
Salt and pepper to taste
1 tablespoon lemon juice
1 teaspoon baking powder
1½ cups milk

Directions

1. Add the bacon to a medium saucepan or skillet and cook over medium heat until evenly crisp and brown. Drain over paper towels and crumble.
2. Preheat the oven to 350°F (177°C). Grease a 12-cup muffin pan with vegetable oil or cooking spray.
3. Beat the eggs in a mixing bowl. Add the flour, milk, spices, and lemon juice. Mix well.
4. Add the baking powder, onions, and cheese. Mix again.
5. Add the crumbled bacon and butter; mix again.
6. Cut the avocado into small pieces. Mix it in with the bowl mixture.

7. Transfer the batter to the muffin pan, filling the liners just ¾ full to allow room for the muffins to rise.
8. Bake for 25 minutes until well set. Check by inserting a toothpick; if it doesn't come out clean, bake for a few more minutes and repeat.
9. Remove from the oven and let the muffins rest in the pan for 5 minutes. Then, transfer to a wire rack to cool down.
10. Gently remove muffins from cups; serve fresh.

Nutrition (per serving)
Calories 144, fat 12 g, carbs 4 g,
Protein 6 g, sodium 481 mg

Avocado Mushroom Egg Muffins

Makes 12 | Prep time 15 minutes | Cooking time 20 minutes

Ingredients

1 avocado, pitted and roughly chopped
10 eggs
3½ ounces champignon mushrooms, roughly chopped
1¾ ounces Parmesan cheese, grated
1¾ ounce cream
1 pinch cayenne pepper (optional)
2 teaspoons black pepper
3 teaspoons salt
1 teaspoon Italian herbs

Directions

1. Preheat the oven to 350°F (177°C). Line a 12-cup muffin pan with parchment paper liners or grease with coconut/olive oil or cooking spray.
2. Add all of the ingredients to a mixing bowl. Mix well.
3. Transfer the batter to the muffin pan, filling the liners just ¾ full to allow room for the muffins to rise.
4. Bake for 20 minutes until the eggs are well set.
5. Remove from the oven and let the muffins rest in the pan for 5 minutes. Then, transfer to a wire rack to cool down.
6. Gently remove muffins from cups; serve fresh.

Nutrition (per serving)

Calories 107, fat 8.5 g, carbs 1.5 g,
Protein 6.5 g, sodium 303 mg

Bacon Egg Muffins

Makes 12 | Prep time 10 minutes | Cooking time 20 minutes

Ingredients
½ teaspoon dry mustard powder
Pepper to taste
2 tablespoons fresh parsley or other herbs
8 slices bacon
12 eggs
⅓ cup heavy cream
2 green onions, chopped
3½ ounces cheddar cheese, shredded
Vegetable oil or cooking spray for greasing

Directions

1. Add the bacon to a medium saucepan or skillet and cook over medium heat until evenly crisp and brown. Drain over paper towels and crumble.
2. Preheat the oven to 375°F (190°C). Grease a 12-cup muffin pan with vegetable oil or cooking spray.
3. Beat the eggs in a mixing bowl. Add the cream, dry mustard, and pepper; mix well.
4. Add the cheese, bacon, and onions evenly over the muffin cups. Sprinkle the parsley on top.
5. Transfer the batter to the muffin pan, filling the liners just ¾ full to allow room for the muffins to rise.
6. Bake for 20–25 minutes until the eggs are well set.
7. Remove from the oven and let the muffins rest in the pan for 5 minutes. Then, transfer to a wire rack to cool down.
8. Gently take the muffins out of the cups; serve fresh.

Nutrition (per serving)

Calories 181, fat 15 g, carbs 1 g
Protein 9 g, sodium 214 mg

Meatloaf Muffins

Makes 12 I Prep time 10 minutes I Cooking time 50 minutes

Ingredients
1 ½ pounds ground beef
½ pound pork sausage, casings removed
1 large egg, lightly beaten
1 onion, diced
1 cup whole milk
1 cup dried breadcrumbs
1 teaspoon red pepper flakes
1 teaspoon salt
½ teaspoon freshly ground black pepper
Cooking spray or butter for greasing

For the topping
2 tablespoons brown sugar
1 tablespoon ground mustard
⅓ cup ketchup

Directions

1. Half an hour before beginning, set out the ground beef and sausage and let it come to room temperature.
2. Preheat the oven to 350°F (177°C) and grease a large muffin pan with cooking spray or butter.
3. In a large bowl, combine all the ingredients for the meatloaf. Press the mixture into lightly greased muffin cups.
4. Bake for 25-30 minutes. Take it out and drain away any grease.
5. In a small mixing bowl, combine the brown sugar, mustard, and ketchup. Mix well and spread it on top of the meatloaf.

6. Return it to the oven until the topping is warmed through, about 5 minutes.

Nutrition per serving
Calories 213, fat 15 g, carbs 9 g,
Protein 10 g, sodium 480 mg

Cheese Parsley Muffins

Makes 6 | Prep time 10 minutes | Cooking time 20 minutes

Ingredients
1 ½ cups all-purpose flour
⅛ teaspoon salt
⅛ teaspoon pepper
1 teaspoon baking powder
1 teaspoon dried parsley
1 cup shredded cheddar cheese
2 eggs, whisked
2 tablespoons salted butter, melted
6 tablespoons heavy cream or half and half
Parsley for sprinkling

Directions

1. Preheat the oven to 400°F (204°C). Grease a 6-cup muffin pan with coconut/olive oil or cooking spray.
2. Add the dry ingredients to a mixing bowl. Mix well.
3. Mix in the shredded cheese.
4. In another large bowl, whisk the egg. Add the cream and butter. Mix well.
5. Combine the mixtures and mix well until no visible lumps remain.
6. Transfer the batter to the muffin pan, filling the liners just ¾ full to allow room for the muffins to rise. Add some parsley on top.
7. Bake for 20 minutes until the muffins turn golden brown. Check by inserting a toothpick; if it doesn't come out clean, bake for a few more minutes and repeat.
8. Remove from the oven and let the muffins rest in the pan for 5 minutes. Then, transfer to a wire rack to cool down.

9. Gently remove muffins from cups; serve fresh.

Nutrition (per serving)
Calories 242, fat 20.5 g, carbs 3 g,
Protein 9 g, sodium 293 mg

Gouda Sausage Muffins

Makes 4 | Prep time 10 minutes | Cooking time 35 minutes

Ingredients

1 pound ground breakfast sausage
3 cups all-purpose baking mix
2 cups Gouda cheese, cut into small cubes
1 cup sour cream
1 cup chicken stock or water
1 teaspoon salt
1 teaspoon black pepper

Directions

1. Preheat oven to 375°F (190°C).
2. In a large skillet, brown the sausage over medium heat until cooked through, approximately 7 minutes.
3. Transfer the sausage to a large bowl and add in the baking mix and Gouda cheese. Mix well.
4. In a smaller bowl, mix the sour cream and chicken stock.
5. Make a well in the center of the sausage mixture and pour the sour cream mixture into the center of it. Slowly incorporate the sour cream mixture while mixing. Season with salt and pepper, if desired.
6. Spoon the sausage mixture into lightly oiled muffin pans. Place in the oven and bake for 25-30 minutes or until golden brown and set in the center.
7. Remove from the oven and let the muffins rest in the pan for 5 minutes. Then, transfer to a wire rack to cool down.
8. Serve warm or slightly cooled.

Nutrition (per serving)

Calories 144, fat 10 g, carbs 1 g,
Protein 13 g, sodium 411 mg

Kale Chives Muffins

Makes 8 | Prep time 10 minutes | Cooking time 30 minutes

Ingredients
¼ cup chives, finely chopped
½ cup almond or coconut milk
6 eggs
1 cup kale, finely chopped
Salt and pepper to taste
8 slices prosciutto or bacon (optional)

Directions

1. Preheat the oven to 350°F (177°C). Grease an 8-cup muffin pan with coconut/olive oil or cooking spray.
2. Line each cup with a slice of prosciutto or bacon.
3. In another large bowl, whisk the eggs. Add the kale and chives. Mix well.
4. Mix in the salt and pepper and almond milk.
5. Evenly distribute the batter among the muffin cups until they are about ⅔ full.
6. Bake for 30 minutes until the eggs are well set and the muffins have risen.
7. Remove from the oven and let the muffins rest in the pan for 5 minutes. Then, transfer to a wire rack to cool down.
8. Gently remove muffins from cups; serve fresh.

Nutrition (per serving)
Calories 177, fat 11 g, carbs 7 g,
Protein 16 g, sodium 485 mg

Jalapeño Cheddar Muffins

Makes 12 | Prep time 15 minutes | Cooking time 30 minutes

Ingredients

2 medium jalapeños
2 teaspoons baking powder
½ teaspoon salt
½ teaspoon garlic powder
2 cups all-purpose flour
¼ cup all-purpose flour
1½ cups shredded cheddar cheese (divided)
6 tablespoons butter, melted
¾ cup almond milk, unsweetened
4 large eggs

Directions

1. Preheat the oven to 325°F (160°C). Line a 12-cup muffin pan with parchment paper liners.
2. Slice the jalapeños crosswise into 12 thin pieces. Dice the remainder into small pieces.
3. Add the all-purpose flour, all-purpose flour, salt, baking powder, and garlic powder to a mixing bowl. Mix well.
4. Add 1 cup of cheese and the diced jalapeños.
5. Add the butter, eggs, and almond milk. Mix well.
6. Transfer the batter to the muffin pan, filling the liners just ¾ full to allow room for the muffins to rise. Top with the jalapeño slices and the remaining cheese.
7. Bake for 30–35 minutes until the muffins turn golden brown. Check by inserting a toothpick; if it doesn't come out clean, bake for a few more minutes and repeat.
8. Remove from the oven and let the muffins rest in the pan for 5 minutes. Then, transfer to a wire rack to cool down.

9. Gently take the muffins out of the cups; serve fresh.

Nutrition (per serving)
Calories 251, fat 21 g, carbs 6 g,
Protein 10 g, sodium 266 mg

Asparagus Cheese Muffins

Makes 12 | Prep time 10 minutes | Cooking time 25 minutes

Ingredients

1 cup asparagus, trimmed and chopped into 1-inch pieces
10 eggs
2 tablespoons olive oil
1 small onion, chopped
½ teaspoon salt (divided)
½ cup chopped parsley
¼ cup plain Greek yogurt
¼ teaspoon pepper
4 ounces goat cheese, crumbled

Directions

1. Preheat the oven to 375°F (190°C). Line a 12-cup muffin pan with parchment paper liners.
2. Heat the olive oil over medium heat in a medium saucepan or skillet.
3. Add the onion, asparagus, and ¼ teaspoon of the salt; stir-cook for 4–5 minutes until softened.
4. Whisk the eggs in a mixing bowl. Add the yogurt, parsley, salt, and pepper; mix well.
5. Add the cooked vegetables and mix again.
6. Transfer the batter to the muffin pan, filling the liners just ¾ full to allow room for the muffins to rise. Add the crumbled goat cheese on top.
7. Bake for 25–30 minutes until the eggs are well set.
8. Remove from the oven and let the muffins rest in the pan for 5 minutes. Then, transfer to a wire rack to cool down.
9. Gently remove muffins from cups; serve fresh.

Nutrition (per serving)
Calories 108, fat 8 g, carbs 1.5 g,
Protein 7 g, sodium 188 mg

Mushroom Chives Muffins

Makes 8 | Prep time 15 minutes | Cooking time 18 minutes

Ingredients

1 cup mushrooms, cut into small pieces
6 medium eggs
1½ tablespoons chives, raw and chopped
⅔ cup cheddar cheese, grated
1 tablespoon olive oil
¼ teaspoon sea salt
⅛ teaspoon pepper
Olive oil

Directions

1. Preheat the oven to 350°F (177°C). Grease an 8-cup muffin pan with coconut/olive oil or cooking spray.
2. Heat the olive oil over medium heat in a medium saucepan or skillet.
3. Add the mushrooms and stir cook for 7–8 minutes until tender. Set aside.
4. In another large bowl, beat the eggs. Add the chives, black pepper, salt, and grated cheese. Mix well.
5. Mix in the mushrooms.
6. Transfer the batter to the muffin pan, filling the liners just ¾ full to allow room for the muffins to rise.
7. Bake for 18–20 minutes until the top turns brown.
8. Remove from the oven and let the muffins rest in the pan for 5 minutes. Then, transfer to a wire rack to cool down.
9. Gently take the muffins out of the cups; serve fresh.

Nutrition (per serving)

Calories 212, fat 16.5 g, carbs 2 g,

Protein 13 g, sodium 266 mg

Cheddar Muffins

Makes 15 | Prep time 15 minutes | Cooking time 12 minutes

Ingredients

2 tablespoons baking powder
4 eggs
3 cups all-purpose flour
½ teaspoon salt
⅔ cup sour cream
½ cup butter, melted
1½ cups cheddar cheese, shredded

Directions

1. Preheat the oven to 400°F (204°C). Grease a 15-cup muffin pan with coconut/olive oil or cooking spray.
2. Add the all-purpose flour, salt, and baking powder to a mixing bowl. Mix well.
3. In another large bowl, whisk the eggs. Add the butter and sour cream. Mix well.
4. Combine the mixtures and mix well until no visible lumps remain.
5. Mix in the cheese.
6. Transfer the batter to the muffin pan, filling the liners just ¾ full to allow room for the muffins to rise.
7. Bake for 12 minutes until the muffins turn golden brown. Check by inserting a toothpick. If it doesn't come out clean, bake for a few more minutes and repeat.
8. Remove from the oven and let the muffins rest in the pan for 5 minutes. Then, transfer to a wire rack to cool down.
9. Gently remove muffins from cups; serve fresh.

Nutrition (per serving)

Calories 264, fat 24 g, carbs 6 g,
Protein 9 g, sodium 227 mg

Ham Red Pepper Muffins

Makes 8 | Prep time 10 minutes | Cooking time 20 minutes

Ingredients

2 tablespoons water
½ pound cooked ham, crumbled
8 eggs
1 cup red bell pepper, seeded and chopped
Salt and ground black pepper to taste
Melted butter (to grease)

Directions

1. Preheat the oven to 350°F (177°C). Grease 8 muffin pans with melted butter.
2. Crack the eggs into a mixing bowl. Add the water, salt, and black pepper; combine well.
3. Add the ham and red bell pepper; combine well.
4. Transfer the mixture to the muffin cups evenly.
5. Bake for about 18–20 minutes or until a toothpick inserted in the center comes out clean.
6. Remove from the oven and let the muffins rest in the pan for 5 minutes. Then, transfer to a wire rack to cool down.
7. Serve warm.

Nutrition (per serving)

Calories 114, fat 7g, carbs 3g,
Protein 11g, sodium 428mg

Spinach, Zucchini, and Prosciutto Muffins

Makes 12 | Prep time 15 minutes | Cooking time 20 minutes

Ingredients
3 garlic cloves, minced
1 bell pepper, finely diced
1 tablespoon olive oil
½ onion, finely diced
¼ cup fresh parsley, roughly chopped
1 cup baby spinach, roughly chopped
Salt and pepper to taste
8 large eggs
2 small zucchinis, thinly sliced
12 slices prosciutto
¼ cup coconut milk or nut milk

Directions

1. Preheat the oven to 350°F (177°C). Grease a 12-cup muffin pan with coconut/olive oil or cooking spray.
2. Line each cup with a slice of prosciutto.
3. Heat the olive oil over medium heat in a medium saucepan or skillet.
4. Add the onion and garlic and stir cook for 1 minute until softened.
5. Add the spinach, sweet pepper, and parsley; stir-cook for 2 minutes until the spinach wilts.
6. Beat the eggs in a bowl. Add the salt and pepper and coconut milk. Mix well.
7. Add the spinach mixture and zucchini. Mix well.
8. Transfer the batter to the muffin pan, filling the liners just ¾ full to allow room for the muffins to rise.
9. Bake for 20 minutes until the eggs are well set.

10. Remove from the oven and let the muffins rest in the pan for 5 minutes. Then, transfer to a wire rack to cool down.
11. Gently take the muffins out of the cups; serve fresh.

Nutrition (per serving)
Calories 107, fat 8 g, carbs 2 g,
Protein 5 g, sodium 101 mg

APPENDIX

Cooking Conversion Charts

1. Measuring Equivalent Chart

Type	Imperial	Imperial	Metric
Weight	1 dry ounce		28g
	1 pound	16 dry ounces	0.45 kg
Volume	1 teaspoon		5 ml
	1 dessert spoon	2 teaspoons	10 ml
	1 tablespoon	3 teaspoons	15 ml
	1 Australian tablespoon	4 teaspoons	20 ml
	1 fluid ounce	2 tablespoons	30 ml
	1 cup	16 tablespoons	240 ml
	1 cup	8 fluid ounces	240 ml
	1 pint	2 cups	470 ml
	1 quart	2 pints	0.95 l
	1 gallon	4 quarts	3.8 l
Length	1 inch		2.54 cm

Numbers are rounded to the closest equivalent

2. Oven Temperature Equivalent Chart

Fahrenheit (°F)	Celsius (°C)	Gas Mark
220	100	
225	110	1/4
250	120	½
275	140	1
300	150	2
325	160	3
350	180	4
375	190	5
400	200	6
425	220	7
450	230	8
475	250	9
500	260	

*   Celsius (°C) = T (°F)-32] * 5/9
**   Fahrenheit (°F) = T (°C) * 9/5 + 32
*** Numbers are rounded to the closest equivalent

Printed in Great Britain
by Amazon

27149731R00137